THE ULTIMATE GUIDE TO RECLAIMING LIFE FROM WORK

Step-by-step Strategies for Liberation from Work's Grip

Ruth Kings

All Rights Reserved. No part of this publication may be produced, stored or transmitted in any form or by any means, electronic, mechanical, photocopying, recording, scanning or otherwise without written permission from the publisher. It is illegal to copy his book, post it to a website, or distribute it by any other means without permission.

Copyright © 2024 RUTH KINGS

TABLE OF CONTENTS.

INTRODUCTION. 7
- WHY WE NEED TO RECLAIM OUR LIVES. 7
- MY JOURNEY - FROM OVERWORKED TO BALANCED. 9

CHAPTER ONE. 15
- UNDERSTANDING THE WORK-LIFE IMBALANCE. 15
- WHAT IS WORK-LIFE BALANCE, REALLY? 15
- THE MYTH OF PERFECT BALANCE. 16
- IDENTIFYING THE SIGNS OF IMBALANCE. 17
- REAL STORIES: HOW WE GOT HERE. 21

CHAPTER TWO. 29
- SETTING YOUR PRIORITIES. 29
- WHAT TRULY MATTERS TO YOU? 29
- THE POWER OF SAYING NO. 31
- ALIGNING YOUR LIFE WITH YOUR VALUES. 34
- EXERCISE TO DISCOVER YOUR PRIORITIES. 36

CHAPTER THREE. 51
- TIME MANAGEMENT TIPS FOR A BALANCED LIFE. 51
- BREAKING DOWN YOUR DAY: FINDING THE GAPS. 51
- CREATING A SCHEDULE THAT WORKS FOR YOU. 53
- THE POMODORO TECHNIQUE AND OTHER HACKS. 55
- HANDLING INTERRUPTIONS GRACEFULLY. 58

CHAPTER FOUR. 65
- CREATING BOUNDARIES. 65
- LEARNING TO UNPLUG: DIGITAL DETOX. 65
- SETTING LIMITS WITH YOUR BOSS AND COLLEAGUES. 69
- PROTECTING FAMILY TIME. 74
- SAYING NO WITHOUT GUILT. 77

CHAPTER FIVE. 87
- SELF-CARE ESSENTIALS. 87

- Why Self-Care is Non-Negotiable. 87
- Finding Time for You: Daily Routines. 89
- Physical Health: Exercise and Nutrition. 93
- Mental Health: Mindfulness and Relaxation Techniques. 97

CHAPTER SIX. 107

- BUILDING A SUPPORT SYSTEM. 107
  - The Importance of Community. 107
  - Finding Your Tribe: Friends and Mentors. 108
  - Leaning on Family for Support. 113
  - Professional Help: When and How to Seek It. 115

CHAPTER SEVEN. 129

- FLEXIBILITY AT WORK. 129
  - Remote Work: Tips and Tricks. 129
  - Negotiating for Better Work Conditions. 132
  - Job Crafting – Making Your Job Work for You. 142

CHAPTER EIGHT. 155

- CULTIVATING HOBBIES AND INTERESTS. 155
  - Rediscovering Old Passions. 155
  - Trying New Things: Expanding Your Horizons 157
  - The Joy of Learning Something New. 161

CHAPTER NINE. 173

- MINDSET SHIFTS FOR A BALANCED LIFE. 173
  - Overcoming the Hustle Culture. 173
  - The Importance of Rest and Play. 176
  - Embracing Imperfection. 184
  - Gratitude and Positivity Practices. 187

CHAPTER TEN. 197

- LONG TERM STRATEGIES FOR SUSTAINABLE BALANCE. 197
  - Setting Long-Term Goals. 197
  - Regular Check-Ins with Yourself. 199
  - Adapting to Life Changes. 200

    CELEBRATING YOUR WINS. 205
CONCLUSION...**215**
    REFLECTING ON YOUR JOURNEY. 215
    CONTINUING TO GROW AND EVOLVE. 216
    ENCOURAGING OTHERS TO RECLAIM THEIR LIVES. 217
    FINAL WORDS OF WISDOM. 218
HOW WAS IT? **221**

INTRODUCTION.
Why We Need to Reclaim Our Lives.

If you're reading this, chances are you've felt that familiar pang of exhaustion, the creeping sense that work is swallowing up more of your life than you ever intended. You're not alone.

In our fast-paced, always-connected world, the line between work and life has become increasingly blurred. But here's the good news: It doesn't have to stay that way.

Let's start with a little story. Picture this: It's a typical Tuesday morning. You wake up to the sound of your alarm, already feeling behind on the day's tasks. Your email notifications ping constantly as you try to get ready. You grab a quick breakfast (if you're lucky) and dive straight into work mode. Before you realize it, hours have flown by. You've skipped lunch, your back is aching, and your eyes are glued to the screen. By the time you shut down your computer, the day feels like a blur. Where did the time go? More importantly, where did your day go?

For many of us, this scenario is all too familiar. We've become so accustomed to this relentless pace that we rarely stop to question it. But what if we did? What if we took a step back and asked ourselves: Is this really how we want to live?

In this book, we're going to thoroughly examine why it's essential to reclaim our lives from the grip of work. We'll dig into the reasons behind our overworked culture and provide practical strategies to find a healthier balance. But before we head into the how, let's take a moment to understand the why. Why do we need to reclaim our lives?

The Cost of Overwork.

First, let's talk about the toll that overworking takes on us. We all know the obvious effects: stress, burnout, and fatigue. But the impact goes much deeper than that. Overworking affects our physical health, our mental well-being, and our relationships. It chips away at our joy and zest for life.

Physically, chronic stress from overwork can lead to a myriad of health issues. High blood pressure, heart disease, and weakened immune systems are just a few of the problems that can arise. When we're constantly in work mode, our bodies never get the chance to fully relax and recover. It's like driving a car without ever stopping for gas—eventually, you're going to break down.

Mentally, the effects can be just as devastating. Anxiety, depression, and a pervasive sense of overwhelm are common. We lose our ability to focus, creativity dwindles, and even simple decisions can become paralyzing. It's hard to feel passionate about anything when you're in a constant state of stress.

And then there are our relationships. How often have you found yourself snapping at a loved one because you're stressed about work? Or missing out on important family moments because you had to finish that project? The people in our lives deserve more than the leftovers of our time and energy.

My Journey - From Overworked to Balanced.

I'm thrilled to have you here because it means you're ready to take a step toward a more balanced and fulfilling life. You're not alone in this journey—many of us have felt the relentless pressure of work creeping into every corner of our lives. In this introduction, I'd like to share my personal story of transitioning from being overworked to finding a balance that brings joy and fulfillment. I hope my journey can serve as both a guide and an inspiration for your own path.

The Early Days: Driven by Ambition.

Let me take you back to the early stages of my career. Fresh out of college, I was filled with ambition and ready to conquer the world. I landed a job at a prestigious marketing firm, which felt like a dream come true. I threw myself into work with unbridled enthusiasm. Long hours didn't bother me—I thrived on the adrenaline of tight deadlines and the satisfaction of a job well done.

For the first few years, this intense dedication seemed to pay off. I received promotions, bonuses, and accolades. My career was on an upward trajectory, and I was proud of my achievements. But there was a cost I hadn't anticipated.

The Subtle Onset of Imbalance.

It started subtly. I missed a few family gatherings here and there, skipped meals, and lost touch with hobbies that once brought me joy. I shrugged it off, telling myself that sacrifices were necessary for success. But as time went on, these sacrifices began to pile up.

My health took a hit. I often felt fatigued, my sleep was disrupted, and I developed chronic headaches. My personal relationships also started to suffer. Friends stopped inviting me out, assuming I was too busy, and I felt a growing distance from my family. Yet, I pushed these concerns aside, believing that hard work and dedication were the only paths to success.

The Breaking Point.

The breaking point came one winter evening. I was working late, again, on a major project. A call came in, and it was from my brother. I ignored it, thinking I'd call him back later. When I finally wrapped up and checked my messages, I saw one from him: "Mom had a heart attack. We're at the hospital."

My heart sank. I rushed to the hospital, guilt and fear gnawing at me. My mother was stable, but the scare was a wake-up call. As I sat by her bedside, I realized how much I had missed. My work had consumed me to the point where I was no longer present for the people who mattered most.

The Decision to Change.

Sitting there in the hospital, I made a decision. I needed to reclaim my life from the overwhelming grip of work. I couldn't continue down this path of relentless stress and constant sacrifice. But, I was clueless about how to begin.

Back at work, I began by reevaluating my priorities. I spoke to my manager about my need for better work-life balance. To my surprise, she was supportive and shared her own struggles with balance. Together, we restructured my workload to allow for more flexibility. I started setting boundaries, like not checking emails after a certain hour and taking regular breaks throughout the day.

The Challenges of Change.

The transition wasn't easy. I felt guilty and anxious at first, worried that I was letting my team down or jeopardizing my career. But I persevered, reminding myself of my commitment to change. I sought advice from mentors, read books on time management and balance, and slowly began to see improvements.

One of the biggest challenges was learning to say no. I had always been a people-pleaser, eager to take on any task thrown my way. But I realized that saying no was essential for my well-being. It allowed me to focus on what truly mattered and perform better in the tasks I did take on.

The Myth of Productivity.

One of the biggest drivers of our overworked culture is the myth of productivity. We've been led to believe that more work equals more success. The more hours we put in, the better we'll perform, and the more we'll achieve. But research tells a different story.

Studies have shown that working long hours doesn't necessarily lead to better outcomes. In fact, after a certain point, our productivity actually decreases. We become less efficient, more prone to errors, and creativity takes a nosedive. It turns out, there's a limit to how much work our brains can handle in a day.

Think about the last time you pulled an all-nighter or worked through the weekend. Did you really get more done? Or did you find yourself staring blankly at your screen, struggling to form coherent thoughts? It's a vicious cycle: we work longer hours to try and get ahead, but in reality, we're just spinning our wheels.

Embracing Flexibility and Finding New Passions.

One of the most significant changes I made was embracing flexibility in my work life. I negotiated a hybrid work arrangement, allowing me to work from home part of the week. This not only reduced my commute time but also gave me more control over my schedule.

With this newfound flexibility, I had more time to explore passions outside of work. I volunteered at a local animal shelter, which brought a sense of purpose and fulfillment. I also started a blog to share my journey and connect with others going through similar struggles. This creative outlet became a source of joy and inspiration.

The Power of Balance.

So, if working more isn't the way out, what is? The key lies in finding balance. It's about creating a life where work is just one part of the equation, not the whole story. It's about making time for the things that bring us joy, nourish our souls, and keep us grounded.

Imagine a day where you wake up feeling rested, with enough time to enjoy your morning coffee without rushing. You start your workday with a clear mind, take regular breaks to recharge, and wrap up at a reasonable hour. You have the energy to go for a walk, spend quality time with your family, or dive into a hobby you love. You go to bed feeling content, knowing that you've given your best at work, but also taken care of yourself.

This balance isn't just a dream—it's entirely possible. And it starts with a shift in mindset. We need to recognize that our worth isn't defined by how many hours we work or how much we achieve. Our value stems from who we are, not what we do.

Taking the First Step.

Reclaiming your life from work isn't about making drastic changes overnight. It's about taking small, intentional steps toward a more balanced life. It's about recognizing that you deserve to live fully, not just exist to work.

In the chapters that follow, we'll explore practical strategies to help you set boundaries, manage your time, and prioritize self-care. We'll look at ways to build a support system and find flexibility in your work arrangements. And we'll go deeper into mindset shifts that can help you break free from the hustle culture and embrace a more fulfilling way of living.

Remember, this is a journey. There will be challenges and setbacks, but every step you take is a step toward a healthier, happier you. So, as we embark on this journey together, let's keep an open mind and a compassionate heart. Let's treat ourselves with kindness and acknowledge our little wins along the way.

A New Way Forward.

As you turn the pages of this book, I hope you find inspiration and practical advice to reclaim your life from the grip of work. I hope you discover new ways to create balance and find joy in the everyday moments. Most of all, I hope you realize that you have the power to make these changes.

We live in a world that often glorifies busyness and equates self-worth with productivity. But it's time to challenge that narrative. It's time to reclaim our lives and redefine success on our own terms. We are more than our jobs. We are friends, family members, creators, dreamers, and so much more.

So, welcome to "The Ultimate Guide to Reclaiming Life from Work." This is your guide to finding balance, joy, and fulfillment. Together, we'll navigate this journey and discover a new way forward. A way that honors our whole selves, not just the part that shows up at work. A way in which we can truly live.

Let's get started!

CHAPTER ONE.
UNDERSTANDING THE WORK-LIFE IMBALANCE.

WHAT IS WORK-LIFE BALANCE, REALLY?

The work-life balance concept is often discussed but rarely unpacked in a way that feels practical and achievable. So, what does work-life balance truly mean? Is it a myth, or can we actually achieve it in our busy lives? Let's explore this together, breaking down the essence of work-life balance and how it can be woven into the fabric of our everyday lives.

The Concept of Work-Life Balance.

At its core, work-life balance is about creating a sustainable equilibrium between the demands of your work life and the needs of your personal life. It's the art of juggling your professional responsibilities with your personal commitments and pleasures. It's not about perfection or dividing your time equally between work and life but about finding a harmonious integration that allows you to thrive in both areas.

Imagine your life as a set of scales. On one side, you have your work—your job, career goals, and professional responsibilities. On the other side, you have your personal life—your family, friends, health, hobbies, and personal interests. The goal is to keep these scales balanced so that neither side overwhelms the other, leading to stress and burnout.

However, balance doesn't mean equal. It's not about spending exactly eight hours at work and eight hours on personal activities every single day. Life is dynamic, and so is balance. Some days, work might demand more of your time and energy, while other days, your personal life might take precedence. True work-life balance is about flexibility and adaptability, not rigid schedules.

Work-life balance means having enough time for work while also ensuring that you have time for relaxation, self-care, and personal activities. It's about finding a rhythm that allows you to meet your professional obligations without sacrificing your personal well-being. This balance is crucial for maintaining your physical health, emotional well-being, and overall happiness.

THE MYTH OF PERFECT BALANCE.

One of the most common misconceptions about work-life balance is the idea of perfect balance. We often hear about achieving the perfect work-life balance, but striving for perfection can set us up for failure and frustration. The truth is, balance looks different for everyone, and it changes over time.

Think of balance as a fluid, ever-changing state rather than a fixed goal. Some weeks, you might find yourself dedicating more time to a big project at work, and that's okay. Other times, you might need to focus more on family events or personal health, and that's okay too. The key is to be mindful of these shifts and make conscious adjustments to avoid long-term imbalance.

The pursuit of perfect balance can lead to unnecessary stress. If you're constantly aiming for an ideal state where everything is perfectly aligned, you might end up feeling guilty or frustrated when life inevitably gets messy. It's important to recognize that life is unpredictable, and balance is about managing these fluctuations with grace and flexibility.

Instead of striving for perfection, aim for a balance that works for you. This means setting realistic expectations and treating yourself with so much kindness. Understand that some days will be more challenging than others, and that's perfectly normal. It's about making the best of your circumstances and prioritizing what matters most at any given moment.

IDENTIFYING THE SIGNS OF IMBALANCE.

Let's start by understanding how to identify the signs of work-life imbalance. Recognizing these signs early can help you take action before things spiral out of control. Here are some common indicators that you might be struggling with an imbalance between work and your personal life:

1. Constant Fatigue:

Feeling tired all the time? This might be a sign that your work-life balance is off. When work takes up too much of your time and energy, it can leave you feeling drained and exhausted, even if you're getting a full night's sleep. You might find yourself relying on caffeine to get through the day or feeling perpetually groggy.

2. Neglected Relationships:

Are you frequently missing family gatherings, social events, or even just quality time with loved ones? If your work is consuming so much of your time that you're unable to maintain your personal relationships, this is a red flag. Neglected relationships can lead to feelings of isolation and loneliness, further exacerbating the stress of work.

3. Health Issues:

Stress-related health problems are another common sign of work-life imbalance. These can include headaches, insomnia, digestive issues, and even more serious conditions like high blood pressure or heart problems. If you're experiencing these health issues, it's crucial to assess whether your work demands are negatively impacting your well-being.

4. Decreased Productivity:

Ironically, working longer hours can sometimes lead to decreased productivity. If you're struggling to focus, feeling less creative, or noticing that your efficiency has dropped, it might be because you're overworking yourself. Productivity isn't just about the number of hours you put in; it's about how effectively you use that time.

5. Loss of Passion:

When work consumes all your time and energy, you might lose interest in hobbies and activities that once brought you joy. This loss of passion can lead to feelings of emptiness and dissatisfaction. If you find that you no longer have the energy or desire to engage in activities you once loved, it's time to reassess your balance.

6. High Stress Levels:

Constant stress and anxiety are clear indicators that something needs to change. If you're feeling overwhelmed, anxious, or constantly on edge, it's a sign that your work-life balance is out of whack. High stress levels can take a serious toll on your mental and physical health, so it's important to address these feelings before they escalate into burnout.

7. Burnout:

Burnout is the ultimate sign of work-life imbalance. It's a state of physical, emotional, and mental exhaustion caused by prolonged stress and overwork. If you're feeling completely depleted, cynical about your job, or unable to find motivation, you might be experiencing burnout. Recognizing burnout early is crucial for taking steps to recover and restore balance in your life.

8. Lack of Personal Time:

If you find that you have little to no time for yourself, it's a clear sign of imbalance. Personal time is essential for self-care, relaxation, and pursuing your interests. Without it, you're likely to feel overwhelmed and unfulfilled. Take note if your days are filled with work tasks and obligations, leaving no room for the things you enjoy.

9. Emotional Instability:

Work-life imbalance can also affect your emotional well-being. You might find yourself experiencing mood swings, irritability, or feelings of sadness and frustration more frequently. If your emotional state is being negatively impacted by work stress, it's important to take steps to address this imbalance.

10. Difficulty Disconnecting:

In today's digital age, it can be absolutely difficult to disconnect from work. If you find yourself constantly checking emails, answering work calls, or thinking about work even when you're off the clock, this is a sign that your work-life balance is suffering. It's essential to set boundaries to ensure you have time to unwind and recharge.

THE ROLE OF SELF-COMPASSION.

Finally, let's talk about the importance of self-compassion in achieving work-life balance. It's easy to be hard on ourselves when we feel like we're not meeting our own expectations or society's standards. But self-compassion is crucial for maintaining a healthy balance.

Being kind to yourself means acknowledging that you're doing your best and that it's okay to have bad days. It's about treating oneself with the same compassion and understanding that you would show a friend.

When you practice self-compassion, you're more likely to make choices that support your well-being and overall balance.

Work-life balance is not about perfection; it's about finding a sustainable way to integrate your work and personal life. It's about being flexible, adaptable, and kind to yourself. Remember, balance is a journey, not a destination. It's an ongoing process of adjustment and self-discovery. By embracing this mindset, you can create a more balanced, fulfilling life.

REAL STORIES: HOW WE GOT HERE.

Now that we've identified the signs of work-life imbalance, let's further look into some real stories that illustrate how people find themselves in this predicament. Hearing these stories can provide valuable insights and perhaps make you feel less alone if you're struggling with similar issues.

Story 1: The Corporate Climber.

Tara had always been ambitious. Fresh out of college, she landed a job at a prestigious marketing firm and quickly climbed the corporate ladder. She was known for her dedication and willingness to put in long hours. Promotions came quickly, but so did the demands of her job.

Tara's typical day started at 6 AM with a quick workout, followed by a commute that allowed her to catch up on emails. Her workday was packed with meetings, presentations, and deadlines. Evenings were often spent finishing up projects or networking at industry events. Weekends? Those were for catching up on work she couldn't get to during the week.

Over time, Tara began to notice changes in her life. She was constantly tired, her friendships were fading, and her health was deteriorating. She couldn't recall the last time she had a vacation. The final straw came when she experienced severe burnout, leading her to take a leave of absence. It was a wake-up call that made her realize the importance of work-life balance. Tara learned to set boundaries and prioritize her well-being, which ultimately made her more effective at work and happier in her personal life.

Story 2: The Entrepreneur.

Michael always dreamed of running his own business. He started a tech startup with a few friends, and the early days were filled with excitement and endless work hours. The startup culture glorified the grind, with everyone pulling all-nighters and working weekends to get the company off the ground.

As the company grew, so did the pressure. Michael found himself working around the clock, juggling investor meetings, product development, and team management. His personal life took a backseat. Relationships suffered, and his health began to decline. He was always on edge, feeling like he couldn't afford to take a break.

One day, Michael had a panic attack in the middle of a meeting. It was a stark reminder that he couldn't keep up this pace indefinitely. Michael realized that to sustain his business and his health, he needed to find balance. He started delegating tasks, setting work hours, and making time for exercise and relaxation. This shift not only improved his well-being but also enhanced his leadership and the overall success of his company.

Story 3: The Working Parent.

Helen is a working mother of two young children. She works full-time as a nurse, a job that is both physically and emotionally demanding. Her days are a blur of early mornings, hectic shifts, and trying to squeeze in time with her kids before bedtime.

Helen often felt guilty—guilty for not spending enough time with her children, guilty for not being able to stay late at work, and guilty for not taking care of herself. She rarely had time for her hobbies or even a moment to relax. The stress was taking a toll on her health, and she found herself becoming increasingly irritable and overwhelmed.

One evening, after a particularly tough day, Helen broke down. She realized she couldn't go on like this. With the support of her family, she decided to make some changes. Helen negotiated a more flexible work schedule, started prioritizing self-care, and sought help with household responsibilities. These adjustments allowed her to be more present with her children and more focused at work, creating a healthier balance.

Story 4: The Remote Worker.

Darwin's job transitioned to remote work during the pandemic. Initially, he loved the flexibility and the extra time saved from not commuting. However, the lines between work and home quickly began to blur. He found himself working longer hours, often late into the night. The lack of a clear boundary between work and personal time made it difficult for him to switch off.

Darwin started experiencing constant fatigue and felt disconnected from his family, even though they were all under the same roof. He missed the social interactions and structure of the office, which had helped him maintain a better work-life balance.

Recognizing the need for change, Darwin set up a dedicated workspace and established clear work hours. He also made a point to take regular breaks and engage in activities that helped him unwind. These steps helped him create a healthier balance between his professional and personal life, making remote work more sustainable.

Story 5: The Caregiver.

Linda's story is a bit different. She is a caregiver for her elderly parents while working full-time as a teacher. Balancing her job with caregiving responsibilities was incredibly challenging. Her days were packed from dawn to dusk, leaving her with little time for herself.

Linda often felt overwhelmed and emotionally drained. The constant juggling act affected her performance at work and her ability to care for her parents effectively. She was caught in a cycle of stress and exhaustion, with no end in sight.

Eventually, Linda reached out for support. She sought help from family members and explored community resources for caregivers. This support network provided her with much-needed relief and allowed her to find a better balance. By taking care of herself, Linda was able to better care for her parents and perform her job more effectively.

Conclusion.

These real stories illustrate the diverse ways in which work-life imbalance can manifest and the profound impact it can have on our lives. Whether you're a corporate professional, an entrepreneur, a working parent, a remote worker, or a caregiver, the struggle to balance work and personal life is universal.

Recognizing the signs of imbalance is the first step towards making meaningful changes. It's essential to be mindful of your well-being and take proactive steps to create a sustainable balance. This might involve setting boundaries, seeking support, prioritizing self-care, and being flexible with your expectations.

Achieving work-life balance is not a one-time task but an ongoing process that requires attention and adjustment. By understanding the signs of imbalance and learning from real stories, you can take steps to reclaim your life from the overwhelming demands of work and create a more fulfilling, balanced life.

Reflection Questions.

1. What Does Balance Look Like for You?

   - Reflect on what an ideal work-life balance means to you personally. What activities or aspects of your life are most important to you outside of work? How do you currently allocate your time between work and personal life, and what changes would you like to make?

2. Recognizing Personal Signs of Imbalance.

- Think about the signs of work-life imbalance discussed in the chapter. In what way have you experienced any of these signs in your own life? Which ones resonate the most with you, and how have they affected your well-being and relationships?

3. Debunking the Myth of Perfect Balance.

- Reflect on the concept of the "perfect" work-life balance. How has this myth influenced your expectations and actions? In what ways can you adjust your mindset to accept a more flexible and realistic approach to balancing work and personal life?

4. Learning from Real Stories.

- Consider the real stories shared in the chapter. Which story did you find most relatable, and why?

What lessons can you take from these stories to apply to your own life and work situation?

Transformative Exercises.

1. Time Audit:

- For one week, keep a detailed log of how you spend your time each day. Include both work and personal activities. At the end of the week, review your log to identify patterns and areas where you might be overcommitting to work or neglecting personal time. Use this insight to make adjustments and create a more balanced schedule.

2. Creating a Vision Board:

- Create a vision board depicting your ideal work-life balance.

Include images, words, and symbols that reflect your personal goals, hobbies, and the type of work environment you desire. Place your vision board somewhere visible to remind yourself of your priorities and motivate you to make positive changes.

3. Setting SMART Goals:

- Establish specific, measurable, attainable, relevant, and time-bound (SMART) goals to improve your work-life balance.

For example, you might set a goal to leave work by 6 PM three times a week to spend more time with family or dedicate one hour each weekend to a personal hobby. Keep track of your progress and make adjustments to your goals as appropriate.

CHAPTER TWO.
SETTING YOUR PRIORITIES.

In our journey to reclaim life from work, understanding and setting your priorities is essential. When you know what truly matters to you, it becomes easier to make decisions that align with your values and goals. This chapter will help you explore what's important to you and harness the power of saying no to create a balanced and fulfilling life.

WHAT TRULY MATTERS TO YOU?

To set your priorities, you first need to identify what truly matters to you. This might sound simple, but in the hustle and bustle of daily life, it's easy to lose sight of your core values and what brings you joy. Here are some steps to help you uncover your true priorities:

1. Reflect on Your Values:

Take some time to reflect on your values. These are the principles and beliefs that influence the decisions you make and the actions you take. Ask yourself questions like:

- What do I stand for?

- What makes me feel fulfilled?

- What am I passionate about?

Write down your thoughts and identify common themes. Your values might include family, health, personal growth, creativity, or community involvement. Understanding your values is the foundation for setting meaningful priorities.

2. Evaluate Your Time and Energy:

Look at how you currently spend your time and energy. Does it align with your values? For a week, keep a journal of your daily activities and how much time you spend on each. This exercise can reveal discrepancies between what you value and where your time goes. You might find that work consumes most of your day, leaving little room for other important aspects of your life.

3. Define Your Goals:

Setting clear goals can help you prioritize your time and efforts.

Consider your goals for your work, relationships, health, and personal growth, among other aspects of your life. Your goals should reflect your true priorities and be consistent with your principles. For example, if family is a top priority, a goal might be to have dinner with your family three times a week.

4. Identify Your Non-Negotiables:

Non-negotiables are the aspects of your life that you're not willing to compromise on. These are the things that are essential to your happiness and well-being. For instance, you might decide that exercising three times a week or spending weekends with your loved ones are non-negotiables. Identifying these can help you make decisions that honor your priorities.

5. Reevaluate Regularly:

Your priorities might change over time, and that's okay. Regularly reevaluate what matters to you and adjust your priorities accordingly. Life is dynamic, and staying flexible will help you adapt to new circumstances while staying true to your values.

THE POWER OF SAYING NO.

Saying no can be incredibly powerful. It allows you to protect your time and energy, focus on what matters, and maintain a healthy balance between work and personal life. However, for many of us, saying no can be challenging. We fear disappointing others, missing out on opportunities, or appearing uncooperative. Here are some strategies to help you harness the power of saying no:

1. Understand Your Limits:

Before you can effectively say no, you need to understand your limits. Be honest with yourself about how much you can handle without compromising your well-being. Knowing your limits helps you make informed decisions about what to take on and what to decline.

2. Prioritize Your Commitments:

When faced with a new request or opportunity, consider your existing commitments and how this new task fits into your priorities. If it aligns with your values and goals, and you have the capacity to take it on, great! If not, it's okay to decline. Prioritizing your commitments ensures that you're dedicating your time and energy to what truly matters.

3. Practice Polite and Firm Responses:

Saying no doesn't have to be harsh or unkind. Practice polite and firm responses that convey your decision clearly. For example:

- "I appreciate the offer, but I'm currently focused on other commitments."

- "Thank you for thinking of me, but I won't be able to take this on at the moment."

- "I'm honored by the opportunity, but I need to prioritize my current projects."

These responses show respect for the other person while asserting your boundaries.

4. *Offer Alternatives:*

If you're unable to help, consider offering alternatives. This might involve suggesting another person who can assist or proposing a different timeline that works better for you. Offering alternatives shows that you're still willing to help in a way that doesn't compromise your priorities.

5. *Use Technology Wisely:*

In today's digital age, technology can both help and hinder our ability to say no. Use tools and apps to manage your time effectively, set reminders, and block out periods for focused work or personal activities. At the same time, be mindful of over-commitment through digital means. It's easy to say yes to virtual meetings and tasks without considering their cumulative impact on your schedule.

6. *Reflect on the Consequences:*

Consider the long-term consequences of saying yes to too many things. Overcommitting can lead to stress, burnout, and a decline in the quality of your work and personal life. Reflecting on these consequences can give you the motivation to say no when necessary.

7. Embrace the Benefits:

Embrace the benefits of saying no. When you protect your time and energy, you can focus on your priorities, achieve your goals, and maintain a healthier work-life balance. Saying no empowers you to live a life that aligns with your values and brings you joy and fulfillment.

ALIGNING YOUR LIFE WITH YOUR VALUES.

To live a fulfilling life, it's essential to align your actions, decisions, and time with your core values. But what does it mean to align your life with your values? Simply put, it means ensuring that your daily activities and long-term goals reflect what is most important to you. Here's how to do it:

1. Identify Your Core Values:

Your core values are the fundamental beliefs that guide your behavior and decisions. They represent what you stand for and what you find most meaningful in life. Common values include family, health, integrity, compassion, creativity, and personal growth. To identify your core values, ask yourself these questions:

- What principles guide my decisions?

- What makes me feel the happiest and most fulfilled?

- What do I stand for, no matter what?

Write down your answers and look for recurring themes. These themes probably represent your core values.

2. Reflect on Your Current Life:

Once you've identified your core values, take a look at how you currently spend your time and energy. Does your daily routine reflect your values? Are your long-term goals aligned with what truly matters to you? For example, if family is a core value, but you're consistently missing family dinners due to work, there's a misalignment that needs to be addressed.

3. Set Goals That Reflect Your Values:

Setting goals that align with your values helps you create a life that is meaningful and fulfilling. Think about what you want to achieve in various aspects of your life, such as in your career, your relationships, your health, and your personal development. Ensure that these goals reflect your core values. For instance, if health is a priority, set a goal to exercise regularly and eat nutritious foods.

4. Make Value-Based Decisions:

When faced with decisions, big or small, consider how they align with your values. This approach can help you stay true to yourself and avoid actions that lead to dissatisfaction. For example, if integrity is a core value, you might decide against a job opportunity that requires compromising your ethical standards.

5. Prioritize Your Time and Energy:

Time and energy are finite resources, and how you allocate them should reflect your values. Prioritize activities and commitments that align with what's most important to you. If creativity is a core value, make time for hobbies and projects that allow you to express yourself artistically.

6. Communicate Your Values:

Share your values with the important people in your life. Communicating your values helps others understand your priorities and can lead to more supportive relationships. For example, if spending quality time with family is important to you, let your employer and colleagues know that you won't be available for work calls during family dinners.

7. Reevaluate and Adjust:

Life is dynamic, and your values may change over time. Regularly reevaluate your values and priorities to ensure they still resonate with you. Adjust your goals and actions as needed to stay aligned with what truly matters.

EXERCISE TO DISCOVER YOUR PRIORITIES.

Discovering your priorities requires introspection and a willingness to explore what truly matters to you. The following exercises can help you identify your priorities and set you on the path to a more balanced life.

1. *The Values Clarification Exercise:*

This exercise helps you identify your core values by reflecting on your past experiences and current beliefs. Here's how to do it:

Step 1: Reflect on Past Experiences

Think about moments in your life when you felt the most fulfilled and happy. What were you doing? Who were you with? Why were these moments meaningful to you? Write down your thoughts.

Step 2: Identify Common Themes

Look for common themes in your reflections. These themes represent your core values. For example, if your happiest moments involve helping others, compassion might be one of your core values.

Step 3: Write Down Your Values

Make a list of the values that most resonate with you. Aim to identify 5-10 core values that reflect what's most important to you.

Step 4: Rank Your Values

Rank your values in order of importance. This step helps you understand which values are non-negotiable and which ones are more flexible.

2. *The Life Wheel Exercise:*

The Life Wheel is a visual tool that helps you assess different areas of your life and identify where you might need to adjust your priorities. Here's how to use it:

Step 1: Draw the Wheel

Draw a circle and divide it into eight parts. Label each segment with a different area of your life, such as career, relationships, health, personal growth, recreation, finances, spirituality, and home environment.

Step 2: Rate Each Area

Rate your satisfaction with each area on a scale from 1 to 10, with 1 being very dissatisfied and 10 being very satisfied. Shade in each segment according to your rating.

Step 3: Analyze the Wheel

Look at your Life Wheel. Which areas are the most and least satisfying? This visual representation can help you see where you need to focus your time and energy to create a more balanced life.

3. *The Priority Matrix:*

The Priority Matrix is a tool that helps you categorize tasks and commitments based on their importance and urgency. Here's how to use it:

Step 1: Draw the Matrix

Draw a four-quadrant grid. Label the quadrants as follows:

- Quadrant 1: Urgent and Important
- Quadrant 2: Important but Not Urgent
- Quadrant 3: Urgent but Not Important
- Quadrant 4: Not Urgent and Not Important

Step 2: List Your Tasks

Write down all your tasks and commitments. Then, categorize them into the appropriate quadrants.

Step 3: Analyze Your Tasks

Focus on tasks in Quadrant 2 (Important but Not Urgent). These tasks align with your long-term goals and values but often get overlooked due to daily urgencies. By prioritizing these tasks, you can make meaningful progress toward your goals and create a more balanced life.

4. The Ideal Day Exercise:

Imagining your ideal day can help you identify what's truly important to you and how you want to spend your time. Here's how to do it:

Step 1: Visualize Your Ideal Day

Close your eyes and visualize your ideal day from the beginning to the end. Where are you? What are you doing? Who are you with? How do you feel?

Step 2: Write Down Your Ideal Day

Write down a detailed description of what your perfect day is. Include everything from your morning routine to how you spend your evenings.

Step 3: Identify Key Elements

Identify the key elements that make your ideal day fulfilling and meaningful. These elements reflect your priorities.

Step 4: Make Adjustments

Compare your ideal day to your current routine. What changes can you make to align your daily life more closely with your ideal day? Start by making small adjustments and gradually incorporate more elements of your ideal day into your routine.

5. The Reflection Journal:

Keeping a reflection journal is a powerful way to discover and reaffirm your priorities over time. Here's how to start:

Step 1: Daily Reflections

Set out a few minutes each day to write in your journal. Reflect on how you spent your day, what activities brought you joy, and what felt like a drain on your energy. Note any moments when you felt particularly aligned or misaligned with your values.

Step 2: Weekly Summaries

At the end of each week, review your daily reflections and write a summary of your week. Identify patterns and recurring themes. Consider how your activities aligned with your core values and goals.

Step 3: Monthly Reviews

Once a month, review your weekly summaries and assess your progress toward living a life aligned with your priorities. Adjust your plans and actions based on your reflections.

6. The Vision Board:

Creating a vision board is a creative way to visualize your priorities and keep them top of mind. Here's how to make one:

Step 1: Gather Supplies

Collect magazines, newspapers, photos, and other visual materials that inspire you. You'll also need a poster board, scissors, glue, and markers.

Step 2: Identify Your Priorities

Reflect on your core values and goals. Think about what you want to prioritize in different areas of your life, such as health, relationships, career, and personal growth.

Step 3: Create Your Vision Board

Cut out images, words, and phrases that represent your priorities and goals. Arrange them on your poster board in a way that feels meaningful to you. Use markers to add any extra words or illustrations.

Step 4: Display Your Vision Board

Place your vision board somewhere you'll see it regularly, such as your bedroom or office. Let it serve as a daily reminder of what's important to you and what you're working toward.

The Power of Priorities in Reclaiming Your Life.

Setting and living by your priorities is transformative. It allows you to take control of your time and energy, focus on what truly matters, and create a life that is fulfilling and balanced. Here's how embracing your priorities can empower you to reclaim your life from work:

1. Increased Fulfillment:

When your actions align with your values, you experience a deeper sense of fulfillment and satisfaction. Activities and goals that reflect your priorities bring more joy and meaning to your life.

2. Reduced Stress:

Focusing on your priorities helps you manage your time and energy more effectively, reducing feelings of overwhelm and stress. You're better equipped to say no to distractions and commitments that don't align with your values.

3. Improved Relationships:

Living by your priorities allows you to invest more time and energy into meaningful relationships. You can nurture connections with family and friends, leading to stronger, more supportive relationships.

4. Enhanced Well-Being:

Prioritizing your health and well-being is essential for a balanced life. When you make time for self-care, exercise, and relaxation, you improve your physical and mental health, leading to a happier, more energetic life.

5. Greater Productivity:

Focusing on your priorities can boost your productivity and efficiency. When you're clear about what matters most, you can set and achieve goals more effectively, both personally and professionally.

6. Personal Growth:

Living by your priorities encourages continuous personal growth. You're more likely to pursue activities and goals that challenge you and help you develop new skills and perspectives.

Conclusion

Setting your priorities and aligning your life with your values is essential for reclaiming your life from work. By understanding what truly matters to you and using exercises to discover and clarify your priorities, you can create a life that is balanced, fulfilling, and reflective of your core values.

Embrace the journey of discovering and living by your priorities. It's a powerful step toward reclaiming your life and creating a future that reflects your true self. As you align your actions, decisions, and time with your values, you'll experience greater fulfillment, reduced stress, improved relationships, enhanced well-being, and continuous personal growth. This is your life, and you have the power to shape it in a way that brings you joy and meaning.

By setting your priorities and living by them, you can reclaim your life from the overwhelming demands of work and create a balanced, fulfilling existence that reflects what truly matters to you. Start today, and take the first step toward a life that is aligned with your values and filled with purpose and joy.

Reflection Questions: What Truly Matters to You?

1. When do you feel most aligned with your true self, and what are you doing during those times?

2. What accomplishments or moments in your life are you most proud of, and what do they reveal about your values?

3. How do you want to be remembered by others, and what legacy do you want to leave behind?

4. If you had unlimited time and resources, how would you choose to spend your days?

Transformative Exercise: The Core Values Inventory

Step 1: List Your Values

Write down at least 20 values that resonate with you. These could include words like family, health, integrity, adventure, creativity, etc.

Step 2: Narrow Down Your List

From your list, choose the ten values that feel most important to you. Then, narrow it down further to your top five core values.

Step 3: Reflect and Prioritize

For each of your top five values, write a short paragraph about why it's important to you and how it influences your decisions and actions. Rank these values in order of priority.

Step 4: Align Your Actions

Reflect on your everyday routines and long-term ambitions. Identify any areas where your actions do not align with your core values and make a plan to adjust.

Reflection Questions: The Power of Saying No

1. What commitments or obligations currently consume most of your time and energy, and are they aligned with your values?

2. How do you feel when you say yes to something you don't truly want to do?

3. What fears or beliefs hold you back from saying no more often?

4. In what areas of your life would saying no create more space for what truly matters to you?

5. How can you practice saying no in a respectful and assertive way?

Transformative Exercise: The Saying No Challenge

Step 1: Identify Your Limits

List out the areas of your life where you feel overwhelmed or stretched too thin. Identify specific commitments or tasks that you could potentially say no to.

Step 2: Practice Saying No

For the next week, commit to saying no to at least one request or obligation that doesn't align with your values or priorities. Start with smaller, less intimidating situations.

Step 3: Reflect on the Experience

After each instance of saying no, reflect on how it felt and what the outcome was. Write about your feelings and any impact it had on your time and energy.

Reflection Questions: Aligning Your Work with Your Values.

1. How does your current job align or misalign with your core values?

2. What aspects of your work bring you the most satisfaction, and why?

3. In what ways does your job enable or hinder your personal growth and development?

4. What changes could you make in your current role to better align with your values?

5. If you could design your ideal job, what would it look like and why?

Transformative Exercise: The Work Alignment Audit

Step 1: Assess Your Current Role

List the tasks, responsibilities, and goals of your current job. Reflect on how each one aligns with your core values and brings you satisfaction.

Step 2: Identify Misalignments

Highlight the aspects of your job that feel misaligned with your values. Consider why these elements are out of alignment and what impact they have on your well-being.

Step 3: Brainstorm Solutions

For each misaligned aspect, brainstorm potential changes or solutions. These could include delegating tasks, altering your approach, or discussing adjustments with your employer.

Step 4: Take Action

Create a plan to implement these changes. Start with small, manageable adjustments and gradually work toward larger, more significant changes. Track your progress and reflect on the impact these changes have on your alignment and satisfaction.

Reflection Questions: Exercises to Discover Your Priorities

1. How do you currently prioritize your time, and how does this reflect your true values?

2. What long-term goals do you have, and how do they align with what truly matters to you?

3. What areas of your life feel neglected, and why?

4. How do you balance short-term demands with long-term priorities?

5. What shifts in your priorities have you noticed over the past year, and what prompted these changes?

Transformative Exercise: The Priority Mapping Exercise

Step 1: List Your Daily Activities

Write down all the activities you engage in on a typical day, including work, household chores, leisure activities, and social interactions.

Step 2: Categorize Your Activities

Categorize each activity based on its alignment with your core values. Use categories such as "highly aligned," "somewhat aligned," and "not aligned."

Step 3: Analyze Your Time Allocation

Analyze how much time you spend on activities in each category. Identify areas where you spend significant time on activities that are not aligned with your values.

Step 4: Reallocate Your Time

Create a new schedule that prioritizes activities highly aligned with your values. Make adjustments to reduce or eliminate time spent on activities that do not align with your priorities.

Step 5: Reflect and Adjust

After a month, reflect on your new schedule. Assess whether you feel more aligned with your values and priorities. Make further adjustments as needed to continue improving your alignment and balance.

CHAPTER THREE.
TIME MANAGEMENT TIPS FOR A BALANCED LIFE.

BREAKING DOWN YOUR DAY: FINDING THE GAPS.

Balancing work and life requires more than just intention; it demands practical strategies that fit your unique lifestyle. In this section, we'll explore how to break down your day to find gaps and create a schedule that truly works for you. Let's look into these time management tips to help you reclaim your life from the overwhelming demands of work.

Understanding where your time goes is the first step in effective time management. By breaking down your day, you can identify gaps and opportunities to make better use of your time. Here's how to do it:

1. Track Your Time:

Start by tracking your daily activities for a week. Use a journal, a spreadsheet, or a time-tracking app to record everything you do, from the moment you wake up until you go to bed. Include work tasks, commuting, meals, breaks, family time, and leisure activities. This exercise will give you a clear picture of how you spend your time.

2. Analyze Your Time Usage:

Once you have a week's worth of data, analyze it to identify patterns and gaps. Are there periods where you're consistently unproductive? Do you spend too much time on specific tasks? Are there chunks of time that could be better utilized? Look for opportunities to streamline your activities and eliminate or reduce time-wasters.

3. Identify Time-Wasters:

Time-wasters are activities that don't contribute to your goals or well-being. These can include excessive social media use, unproductive meetings, and procrastination. Identifying these time-wasters is crucial for creating more productive and balanced days. Consider setting limits on these activities or finding ways to eliminate them altogether.

4. Batch Similar Tasks:

Grouping similar tasks together can save time and increase efficiency. For example, set specific times for checking emails, making phone calls, or completing administrative tasks. This approach, known as task batching, minimizes the time lost in switching between different activities and helps you stay focused.

5. Schedule Breaks and Downtime:

Breaks are essential for maintaining productivity and well-being. Plan regular breaks throughout the day to relax and recharge. Use this time for activities that relax and rejuvenate you, such as a short walk, stretching, or a quick meditation session. Remember, downtime is just as important as work time for maintaining a balanced life.

6. Categorize Activities:

After tracking your time, categorize your activities. Group them into categories such as work, personal care, family time, social activities, chores, and leisure. This helps you see how much time you're dedicating to each area of your life.

7. Identify Patterns:

Look for patterns in your time usage. Are there certain times of the day when you're most productive? Are there periods when you tend to procrastinate or waste time? Understanding these patterns can help you optimize your schedule.

CREATING A SCHEDULE THAT WORKS FOR YOU.

Now that you've identified the gaps in your day and eliminated time-wasters, it's time to create a schedule that supports a balanced life. Here's how to design a schedule that works for you:

1. Set Clear Goals:

Start by defining your short-term and long-term goals. What do you hope to achieve in both your personal and professional life? Clear goals will help you prioritize tasks and allocate time effectively.

2. Design Your Ideal Day:

Think about what your ideal day looks like. What time do you wake up? How do you spend your morning? What activities make you feel energized and fulfilled? Use this vision as a guide to create a daily schedule that aligns with your values and priorities.

3. Block out Time for High-Priority Tasks:

Identify your most important tasks and block out dedicated time for them. This might include work projects, exercise, family time, or personal development. Schedule these high-priority tasks during your most productive hours, whether that's early in the morning, late at night, or somewhere in between.

4. Create a Morning Routine:

A consistent morning routine can set a positive tone for the rest of your day. Incorporate activities that energize and inspire you, such as exercise, meditation, reading, or a healthy breakfast. A well-structured morning routine can boost your productivity and help you start the day with a clear mind.

5. Plan Your Day the Night Before:

Take a few minutes each evening planning the next day. Review your goals, prioritize your tasks, and create a to-do list. Planning ahead reduces decision fatigue and helps you start the day with a sense of purpose and direction.

6. Be Realistic About Your Time:

It's easy to overestimate your daily productivity. Be realistic about how much time is required for each task and avoid overloading your schedule. Leave buffer time between tasks to accommodate unexpected interruptions or delays.

7. Balance Work and Personal Activities:

Ensure your schedule includes a healthy mix of work and personal activities. Allocate time for work tasks, but also make sure to schedule time for hobbies, socializing, and relaxation. A balanced schedule promotes well-being and prevents burnout.

THE POMODORO TECHNIQUE AND OTHER HACKS.

Let's go right into a game-changing method that can transform how you manage your time: the Pomodoro Technique. This isn't just another productivity hack—it's a strategy that can help you focus, get more done, and even sneak in some much needed breaks.

The Pomodoro Technique: A Breakdown

The Pomodoro Technique, developed by Francesco Cirillo in the late 1980s, is named after the tomato-shaped kitchen timer that Cirillo used during his university days. Here's how it works:

1. Choose a Task: Pick a task you want to work on. It can be anything from writing an email to preparing a presentation.

2. Start a Timer: Start a timer for 25 minutes. This period of time is known as one "Pomodoro."

3. Work: Focus solely on your task until the timer rings. If you think of something else you need to do, jot it down quickly and get back to your task.

4. Short Break: When the timer rings, take a 5-minute break. Stand up, stretch, grab a coffee—whatever helps you refresh.

5. Repeat: After four Pomodoros, take a longer break, about 15-30 minutes. This helps your brain recharge before the next round.

The beauty of the Pomodoro Technique is its simplicity and efficacy. By breaking work into manageable intervals, you maintain high levels of focus and avoid burnout. The regular breaks keep your mind fresh and your motivation high.

Why the Pomodoro Technique Works.

The Pomodoro Technique works on several levels:

- Prevents Burnout: Regular breaks prevent the exhaustion that comes from long, uninterrupted work sessions.
- Improves Focus: Knowing you have only 25 minutes can make you more motivated to avoid distractions and stay on task.

- Encourages Flow: Short bursts of work can help you enter a state of flow more easily, where you become fully immersed in what you're doing.
- Tracks Progress: You can measure your productivity in Pomodoros, which provides a clear sense of accomplishment.

Other Effective Time Management Hacks.

While the Pomodoro Technique is powerful, it's not the only tool in the time management arsenal. Here are some other hacks that can help you manage your time more effectively:

1. Time Blocking:

Time blocking involves allocating certain blocks of time for various tasks or activities. Here's how to do it:

- **Identify Tasks:** List out all the tasks you need to accomplish.
- **Assign Blocks:** Allocate specific time slots for each task. For example, you might reserve 9-11 AM for deep work and 1-2 PM for meetings.
- **Stick to the Schedule:** Treat these time blocks as appointments with yourself. Avoid multitasking and concentrate entirely on the work at hand for each block.

Time blocking helps you manage your day more intentionally and ensures that important tasks get the attention they deserve.

2. The Two-Minute Rule:

The two-minute rule is straightforward: if a task takes less than two minutes to perform, do it right away. This prevents small tasks from piling up and taking up mental space. For instance, replying to a quick email or putting away a dish can be done instantly rather than adding it to your to-do list.

3. The 80/20 Rule (Pareto Principle):

According to the Pareto Principle, 80% of your results come from 20% of your efforts. Identify the 20% of tasks that yield the most significant results and focus on those. This helps you work smarter, not harder.

Handling Interruptions Gracefully.

Interruptions are inevitable, but how you handle them can make a significant difference in maintaining your productivity and balance. Let's explore strategies to manage interruptions effectively:

1. Anticipate and Plan for Interruptions

- Identify Common Interruptions
- Start by identifying the most common interruptions you face. These might include phone calls, emails, colleague drop-ins, or family demands. Knowing what to expect allows you to plan and mitigate these disruptions.

2. Set Boundaries and Communicate Them

Establishing clear boundaries is crucial. Here's how:

- Create a Signal: Use a signal to indicate when you're in focused work mode. This could be closing your office door, using a "do not disturb" sign, or wearing headphones.
- Communicate Expectations: Let those around you know your boundaries. Explain when you're available and when you need uninterrupted time. Clear communication helps others respect your focus time.

3. Schedule Interruption Time

- Allocate specific times in your schedule for handling potential interruptions. For instance, set times for checking emails or returning calls. This way, you can address interruptions without letting them derail your entire day.

Techniques to Manage Interruptions:

1. The 5-Minute Rule:

When an interruption occurs, assess if it can be addressed within five minutes. If so, handle it quickly and move on. If it will take longer, schedule it for later and return to your task.

2. Use a Parking Lot:

Keep a "parking lot" list for non-urgent interruptions. When someone interrupts with a question or request, jot it down in your parking lot and address it during your scheduled interruption time. This keeps you on track and ensures nothing gets forgotten.

3. Practice Assertive Communication:

Assertive communication involves being clear and direct while remaining respectful. Here's how to do it:

- ***Acknowledge the Interruption:*** Politely acknowledge the person or interruption.
- ***Express Your Need:*** Clearly state that you need to focus and will address their concern later. For example, "I'm in the middle of a focused task right now. Can we discuss this at 2 PM?"
- ***Follow Through***: Make sure to follow up at the designated time. This builds trust and shows respect for the other person's needs.

4. Set Up Physical and Digital Barriers:

Physical and digital barriers can help minimize interruptions:

- Physical Barriers: Create a dedicated workspace where you can close the door or use visual cues to signal that you're busy.
- Digital Barriers: Use tools like email filters, do-not-disturb settings on your phone, and apps that block distracting websites during work hours.

Training Others to Respect Your Time.

Teaching others to respect your time is a crucial step in managing interruptions. Here's how to do it effectively:

1. Lead by Example:

Demonstrate good time management practices yourself. When others see you respecting your own time and theirs, they're more likely to reciprocate.

2. Be Consistent:

Consistency is key. If you set boundaries and communicate them clearly, stick to them. Consistency builds habits and reinforces the importance of respecting time.

3. Educate and Collaborate:

Sometimes, others may not understand the impact of their interruptions. Take the time to educate colleagues, family members, or friends about your need for focused work periods. Team up to find solutions that work for everyone.

Dealing with Unexpected Interruptions.

Despite your best efforts, unexpected interruptions will still occur. Here's how to handle them gracefully:

1. Stay Calm and Patient:

Unexpected interruptions can be frustrating, but staying calm and patient helps you handle them more effectively. Take a deep breath and address the situation without letting it derail your focus.

2. Reassess Priorities:

When an unexpected interruption arises, reassess your priorities. Determine if the interruption is urgent or can wait. Adjust your schedule accordingly to accommodate the most critical tasks.

3. Embrace Flexibility:

Flexibility is essential in managing interruptions. Life is unpredictable, and being adaptable helps you navigate disruptions without losing momentum. Embrace a mindset that allows for adjustments and changes.

Conclusion.

Managing your time effectively is a crucial component of achieving a balanced life. By implementing strategies like the Pomodoro Technique and other time management hacks, you can enhance your productivity and ensure that you're dedicating time to what truly matters.

Handling interruptions gracefully is equally important. By anticipating and planning for interruptions, setting boundaries, and using assertive communication, you can minimize disruptions and maintain focus. Remember, effective time management is a skill that can be improved with practice. Be patient with yourself and continually refine your approach.

Ultimately, finding a balance between work and personal life is a journey. Embrace these strategies, adapt them to your unique needs, and enjoy the benefits of a more harmonious and fulfilling life.

Breaking down Your Day: Finding the Gaps

Reflection Question 1:

How do you currently spend your time each day? Are there any patterns or routines that stand out?

Transformative Exercise 1:

Time Audit: For one week, keep a detailed log of how you spend your time each day. Note down each activity, no matter how small, and the duration. At the end of the week, review your log and identify patterns, time-wasting activities, and potential gaps where you could be more productive or insert self-care activities.

Creating a Schedule that Works for You

Reflection Question 2:

What are your most productive times of the day? When do you feel most energized and focused?

Transformative Exercise 2:

Optimal Schedule Creation: Using the insights from your time audit, create a weekly schedule that aligns with your natural energy levels and productivity peaks. Block out time for your most important tasks during your peak hours and schedule less demanding activities for times when your energy is lower. Ensure to include breaks and personal time in your schedule.

The Pomodoro Technique and Other Hacks

Reflection Question 3:

How do you currently manage your tasks and breaks? Do you often feel overwhelmed or distracted?

Transformative Exercise 3:

Pomodoro Trial: Implement the Pomodoro Technique for one week. Start a timer for 25 minutes and concentrate solely on a single task until the timer rings.

Then, take a 5-minute break. After four Pomodoros, take an extended break of 15-30 minutes. At the end of the week, reflect on how this method affected your focus, productivity, and stress levels. Adjust the length of your Pomodoros and breaks as needed to fit your work style.

Handling Interruptions Gracefully

Reflection Question 4:

What are the most common interruptions you face during your workday? How do these interruptions impact your productivity and stress levels?

Transformative Exercise 4:

Interruption Management Plan: Identify the top three sources of interruptions in your day. For each source, develop a specific strategy to handle it. This could include setting clear boundaries, using a "do not disturb" sign, or scheduling specific times to address these interruptions. Implement these strategies for one week and evaluate their effectiveness in reducing interruptions and improving focus.

CHAPTER FOUR.
CREATING BOUNDARIES.

Balancing work and life often feels like a tightrope walk. One of the keys to finding that balance lies in creating and maintaining boundaries. These boundaries are essential for preserving your well-being, productivity, and overall happiness. Let's explore two critical aspects of boundary-setting: learning to unplug with a digital detox and setting limits with your boss and colleagues.

LEARNING TO UNPLUG: DIGITAL DETOX.

In today's hyper-connected world, unplugging can seem like an impossible task. Our smartphones, laptops, and other devices are constantly pinging with notifications, emails, and social media updates. While technology has undoubtedly made our lives easier in many ways, it has also blurred the lines between work and personal life. Learning to unplug and engage in a digital detox can help restore these boundaries and improve your mental health.

Why a Digital Detox Matters.

Imagine waking up in the morning and, instead of reaching for your phone to check emails or social media, you take a few moments to stretch, breathe deeply, and enjoy the quiet start to your day. A digital detox is about reclaiming these moments and reducing the constant bombardment of digital stimuli.

1. Reducing Stress and Anxiety:

Constant connectivity can lead to increased stress and anxiety. Every time your phone buzzes, your brain gets a small jolt of adrenaline, which, over time, can leave you feeling constantly on edge. By setting aside time to disconnect, you allow your brain to relax and recharge.

2. Improving Sleep Quality:

The blue light emitted by screens can interfere with your sleep patterns by suppressing the production of melatonin, the hormone responsible for regulating sleep. Unplugging from your devices at least an hour before bed can improve the quality of your sleep, leaving you feeling more rested and energized.

3. Enhancing Focus and Productivity:

Multitasking and constant notifications can fragment your attention, making it difficult to concentrate on any one task. By engaging in a digital detox, you can reclaim your focus and become more productive in both your work and personal life.

Steps to a Successful Digital Detox.

1. Set Clear Goals:

Determine what you hope to achieve with your digital detox. Are you looking to reduce stress, improve sleep, or simply take a break from the constant influx of information? Having clear goals can help you stay committed to the process.

2. Create Tech-Free Zones:

Decide which areas specific areas of your house are off-limits to technology. The bedroom, dining room, and living room are great places to start. By keeping these spaces free of digital devices, you create an environment conducive to relaxation and quality time with loved ones.

3. Schedule Unplugged Time:

Set aside dedicated periods of time every day or week to unplug. This could be an hour before bed, during meals, or a designated day of the week. Use this time to engage in activities that don't involve screens, such as reading a book, going for a walk, or spending time with family and friends.

4. Use Technology to Your Advantage:

Ironically, technology can help you unplug. There are numerous apps available that can help you manage your screen time, set usage limits, and remind you to take breaks. Apps like "Forest" and "Moment" are designed to help you stay focused and reduce your reliance on digital devices.

CREATING RITUALS TO DISCONNECT.

Creating rituals around disconnecting from technology can help reinforce the habit and make it easier to stick with over time.

1. *Morning Rituals:*

Start your day without immediately diving into emails or social media. Instead, create a morning ritual that helps you ease into the day. This could include activities like stretching, meditating, enjoying a cup of coffee or tea, or taking a short walk. These activities help you start your day with intention and calmness, setting a positive tone for the hours ahead.

2. *Evening Rituals:*

Just as a morning ritual can help you start your day right, an evening ritual can help you wind down. Turn off all screens at least an hour before bed and engage in relaxing activities such as reading a book, practicing gentle yoga, or taking a bath. This signals to your brain that it's time to relax and prepare for sleep.

3. *Weekend Rituals:*

Designate certain weekends or even specific days as tech-free. Use this time to reconnect with nature, spend quality time with loved ones, or pursue hobbies that don't involve screens. These regular breaks can significantly reduce stress and enhance your overall well-being.

The Power of Mindfulness in Digital Detox.

Mindfulness practices can complement your digital detox efforts by helping you stay present and reduce the urge to constantly check your devices.

1. Mindful Breathing:

Spend a few time each day practicing mindful breathing. Focus on your breath as it enters and leaves your body, and let go of any distractions. This simple practice can help you become more aware of your digital habits and make it easier to resist the urge to reach for your phone.

2. Mindful Walking:

Engage in mindful walking by paying attention to the sensations of each step, the sounds around you, and the feeling of the ground beneath your feet. This practice can be especially effective if done outdoors, as it allows you to connect with nature and take a break from screens.

3. Mindful Eating:

Practice mindful eating by savoring each bite of your meal, noticing the flavors, textures, and aromas. Turn off all screens during meals and focus solely on the experience of eating. This not only enhances your enjoyment of food but also helps you disconnect from technology.

SETTING LIMITS WITH YOUR BOSS AND COLLEAGUES.

Creating boundaries isn't just about managing your personal time—it's also about setting clear limits at work. This can be particularly challenging if you're dealing with demanding bosses or colleagues who expect you to be available around the clock. However, setting these boundaries is crucial for maintaining a healthy work-life balance.

1. *Communicate Clearly and Assertively:*

Setting boundaries at work requires effective communication. This involves clearly articulating your needs and expectations in a respectful and assertive manner. Here are some tips:

Be Honest About Your Capacity:

a. If you're feeling overwhelmed with your workload, let your boss or colleagues know. Politely but firmly explain that you have reached your capacity and cannot take on additional tasks without compromising the quality of your work. For example, you might say, *"I understand this project is important, but I need to finish my current tasks before I can take on anything new."*

b. ***Set Expectations for Availability:*** It's important to establish clear expectations about your availability. Let your boss and colleagues know when you are and aren't available for work-related matters. You could say for example, "My availability for work-related communication is from 9 AM to 6 PM". Outside of these hours, I will not be checking emails or taking work calls unless it's an emergency."

c. **Use "I" Statements:** When setting boundaries, use "I" statements to express your needs without sounding accusatory or confrontational. For example, "I need to focus on this project without interruptions for the next two hours" is more effective than "You keep interrupting me."

2. Prioritize and Delegate:

Setting boundaries also means prioritizing your tasks and delegating when necessary. Here's how to do it:

a. **Prioritize Tasks:** Prioritize the tasks that are most important to you and focus on those first. Sort tasks into priority and urgency groups using tools such as Eisenhower Matrix. This helps you manage your time more effectively and ensures that you're focusing on high-priority work.

b. **Delegate When Possible:** If you have too much on your plate, consider delegating some tasks to colleagues or team members. Delegation not only helps lighten your load but also empowers others and fosters a collaborative work environment.

3. Establishing Physical and Virtual Boundaries:

Creating physical and virtual boundaries can help you maintain a clear separation between work and personal life.

- **a. Create a Dedicated Workspace:** If you're working from home, set up a dedicated workspace that is separate from your living areas. This helps create a physical boundary between work and personal life, making it easier to "leave" work at the end of the day.
- **b. Set Office Hours:** Establish and communicate your office hours to your boss and colleagues. Stick to these hours as much as possible to maintain a clear boundary between work time and personal time.

4. Building a Supportive Work Culture:

Creating a culture that respects boundaries starts with leading by example and encouraging others to do the same.

- **a. Lead by Example:** If you're in a position of leadership, set a good example for your team. Respect others' boundaries by not sending emails or messages outside of work hours and encouraging them to take breaks and vacations.
- **b. Encourage Open Communication:** Foster an environment where team members feel comfortable discussing their boundaries and workload. Encourage regular check-ins to discuss workloads, challenges, and how to support each other better.

5. Handling Pushback:

Setting boundaries can sometimes lead to push back from bosses or colleagues who are used to having constant access to you. Here's how to handle it:

- **a. *Stay Firm:*** While it's important to be respectful, it's equally important to stay firm in your boundaries. Reiterate your needs and the reasons behind them.
- **b. *Offer Solutions:*** If your boss or colleague is resistant to your boundaries, try to offer solutions that address their concerns. For example, if they need updates outside of work hours, suggest setting up regular check-in meetings during work hours to keep them informed.

Creating and maintaining boundaries is essential for achieving a balanced life. Whether it's learning to unplug through a digital detox or setting limits with your boss and colleagues, these boundaries protect your well-being and productivity. Remember, setting boundaries is not about being rigid or uncooperative; it's about creating a sustainable work-life balance that allows you to thrive both personally and professionally.

Dealing with Resistance.

Setting boundaries can sometimes be met with resistance, especially if your workplace culture doesn't prioritize work-life balance.

1. Stay Calm and Assertive:

When faced with resistance, stay calm and assertive. Reiterate your boundaries and explain why they are important for your well-being and productivity. For example, you might say, "I understand this is urgent, but maintaining my work-life balance is essential for my overall performance. I will address this first thing tomorrow."

2. *Offer Compromises:*

If your boss or colleagues are resistant to your boundaries, try to find a compromise that addresses their concerns while still respecting your limits. For example, you might agree to check emails once in the evening but not respond to non-urgent matters until the next workday.

3. *Seek Support from HR or Mentors:*

If resistance persists, seek support from HR or a trusted mentor. They can provide guidance on how to navigate the situation and help advocate for your boundaries. HR can also mediate discussions if necessary, ensuring that your rights and well-being are respected.

When you take these steps, you'll not only improve your own well-being but also contribute to a more balanced and respectful work environment for everyone around you. So take the leap, set those boundaries, and start reclaiming your life from work today.

Protecting Family Time.

In our increasingly busy lives, protecting family time can feel like a constant battle. We often find ourselves torn between the demands of work and the desire to spend quality time with our loved ones. However, creating boundaries that prioritize family time is essential for maintaining healthy relationships and ensuring personal well-being. Let's examine how you can protect family time and make it a sacred part of your routine.

Understanding the Importance of Family Time.

Before going into practical strategies, it's crucial to understand why family time is so important. Spending quality time with family provides numerous benefits, including:

- **Strengthening Bonds:** Regular family time fosters stronger relationships and deeper connections with your loved ones. It helps build trust, communication, and a sense of belonging.

- **Creating Lasting Memories:** Shared experiences create lasting memories that enrich our lives. These memories become cherished moments that we can look back on with fondness.

- **Enhancing Mental and Emotional Well-being:** Spending time with family can reduce stress, improve mood, and provide emotional support. It acts as a buffer against the pressures of work and daily life.

- **Modeling Work-Life Balance:** Demonstrating the importance of family time sets a positive example for your children and encourages them to prioritize their own well-being in the future.

Practical Strategies for Protecting Family Time.

Now that we understand the significance of family time, let's explore practical strategies to protect it:

1. Schedule Family Time like an Appointment:

Treat family time as you would any important work meeting or appointment. Block out specific times in your calendar for family activities and stick to them. By scheduling family time, you send a clear message that it is a priority.

2. Create Family Rituals:

Establishing family rituals can create a sense of routine and anticipation. These rituals can be simple yet meaningful, such as:

- **Family Dinners:** Make it a habit to have dinner together as a family as often as possible. Use this time to catch up on each other's day, share stories, and enjoy a meal together.
- **Weekend Activities:** Plan regular weekend activities that the whole family can look forward to. This could be a weekly game night, a hike, a movie night, or a visit to a local park.
- **Daily Check-Ins:** Set aside a few minutes each day for a family check-in. This could be a brief chat before bedtime or during breakfast to discuss everyone's plans and feelings.

3. Limit Work Intrusions:

To protect family time, it's essential to set clear boundaries around work-related activities. This includes:

- **Turning Off Notifications:** During family time, turn off work-related notifications on your phone and other devices. This minimizes distractions and allows you to be fully present with your family.
- **Setting Work Hours:** Establish specific work hours and communicate them to your colleagues and clients. Make it clear when you will be available for work-related matters and when you will not.
- **Creating a Separate Workspace:** If possible, create a designated workspace in your home where you can focus on work. This physical separation can help you mentally switch between work and family time.

4. Delegate and Share Responsibilities:

Sharing responsibilities can help free up more time for family. Delegate tasks at work and share household chores with your partner and children. This not only lightens your load but also fosters a sense of teamwork and cooperation within the family.

SAYING NO WITHOUT GUILT.

One of the most challenging aspects of creating boundaries is learning to say no without feeling guilty. We often worry about disappointing others or missing out on opportunities. However, saying no is a vital skill for protecting our time, energy, and well-being. Let's take a look at different ways to say no with confidence and without guilt.

The Power of Saying No.

Saying no is a powerful act of self-care and boundary-setting. Here are some of the reasons why it's important:

1. **Protects Your Time and Energy:** Saying no to additional commitments allows you to focus on what truly matters to you, whether it's family time, self-care, or personal projects.

2. **Empowers You:** Saying no reinforces your autonomy and control over your own life. It reminds you that you have the right to prioritize your needs and well-being.

3. **Enhances Relationships:** When you say no to commitments that don't align with your priorities, you can devote more time and energy to meaningful relationships and activities.

Strategies for Saying No.

Learning to say no gracefully and confidently takes practice. Here are some ideas to help you learn this essential skill:

1. Clarify Your Priorities:

Before you can say no effectively, it's important to clarify your priorities. Spend some time reflecting on what is most important to you. What are your core values? What goals are you working towards? By understanding your priorities, you can make more informed decisions about where to invest your time and energy.

2. Be Honest and Direct:

When saying no, honesty and directness are key. Extensive justifications or apologies are not needed. A simple, clear response is often the best approach. For example:

- *"Thank you for thinking of me, but I won't be able to take on this project at the moment."*

- *"I appreciate the invitation, but I have other commitments that I need to prioritize."*

- *"I'm unable to help with this task, but I can recommend someone else who might be available."*

3. Use Positive Language:

Frame your response in a positive way to soften the impact of your no. This can help maintain a positive tone and reduce any potential disappointment. For example:

- *"I'm honored that you thought of me, but I'm currently focused on other projects that require my full attention."*

- *"I would love to help in the future, but right now, I need to focus on my existing commitments."*

4. Offer Alternatives:

If possible, offer alternatives or solutions when you say no. This shows that you still want to be helpful, even if you can't take on the task yourself. For example:

- "I'm unable to take on this project, but I can recommend someone else who might be a good fit."

- "I'm not able to attend the meeting, but I can provide some suggestions via email beforehand."

5. Rehearse Your Responses:

If you find it difficult to say no in the moment, rehearse your responses in advance. Rehearse in front of your mirror or with a friend. The more you practice, the more confident and comfortable you'll become in setting boundaries.

Overcoming the Fear of Disappointing Others.

A common barrier to saying no is the fear of disappointing others. We worry about how our refusal will be received and whether it will affect our relationships or reputation. Here are some suggestions to help you get over this fear:

1. Shift Your Perspective:

Instead of focusing on the potential disappointment of others, shift your perspective to the positive impact of saying no. By setting boundaries, you're ensuring that you have the time and energy to fulfill your existing commitments and take care of yourself. This, in turn, allows you to show up more fully for the people and activities that matter most to you.

2. Recognize Your Limits:

Understand that you have limits and that it's impossible to please everyone all the time. Acknowledge that it's okay to have boundaries and that saying no is a necessary part of maintaining your well-being.

3. Communicate Your Reasons:

When appropriate, communicate your reasons for saying no. This can help others understand your perspective and reduce any potential disappointment. For example:

- *"I have a lot on my plate right now and need to prioritize my current projects."*

- *"I'm focusing on spending more time with my family, so I'm unable to take on additional duties."*

4. Trust Your Decision:

Have faith that you're doing what's best for you. Remember that you have the right to prioritize your needs and well-being. Trust that those who care about you will understand and respect your boundaries.

Conclusion.

Setting boundaries is not about being selfish or uncooperative. It's about honoring your own needs and creating a sustainable approach to work and life. As you practice these techniques, you'll find that you have more energy, better relationships, and a greater sense of fulfillment. Embrace the journey of setting boundaries, and watch how it transforms your life for the better.

Reflection Questions: Learning to Unplug: Digital Detox

1. Current Digital Habits: How much time do you spend on digital devices each day, and how does it impact your overall well-being and productivity?

2. Emotional Triggers: What emotions or triggers prompt you to reach for your digital devices, and how can you address them in healthier ways?

3. Quality of Connections: How does your digital usage affect the quality of your connections with family, friends, and colleagues?

4. Benefits of Unplugging: What positive changes have you noticed when you have taken a break from digital devices in the past?

Transformative Exercises:

1. Digital Detox Plan: Create a personalized digital detox plan. Include specific times of the day when you will unplug, activities you will engage in during that time, and strategies to stay committed.

2. Tech-Free Zones: Designate certain areas of your home as tech-free zones. Spend time in these areas engaging in offline activities such as reading, cooking, or spending time with family.

3. Mindful Use of Technology: Practice mindful use of technology by setting a timer for your digital activities. When the timer goes off, take a break and engage in a non-digital activity for at least 15 minutes.

Reflection Questions: Setting Limits with Your Boss and Colleagues

1. Current Boundaries: What boundaries, if any, have you already set with your boss and colleagues, and how effective have they been?

2. Work-Life Balance: How does your current work situation impact your work-life balance, and what changes would you like to see?

3. Communication Style: How comfortable are you with communicating your boundaries, and what challenges do you face in doing so?

4. Long-Term Goals: What long-term goals do you have for your career and personal life, and how can setting limits help you achieve them?

Transformative Exercises:

1. Boundary Inventory: Make a list of boundaries you need to set with your boss and colleagues. Prioritize them based on urgency and impact on your well-being.

2. Role-Playing: Practice role-playing scenarios with a trusted friend or family member where you assert your boundaries in a respectful and confident manner.

3. Boundary Setting Plan: Develop a plan for setting boundaries at work. Outline specific steps, including how you will communicate your boundaries, anticipate potential challenges, and strategies to overcome them.

Reflection Questions: Protecting Family Time

1. Family Priorities: What are your top priorities when it comes to family time, and how well are you currently meeting them?

2. Quality vs. Quantity: How do you balance the quality and quantity of time spent with your family, and what improvements can be made?

3. Family Rituals: What family rituals or traditions do you currently have, and how do they contribute to your family's sense of connection and well-being?

4. Work Intrusions: How often does work intrude on your family time, and what strategies can you implement to minimize these intrusions?

Transformative Exercises:

1. Family Time Audit: Conduct a family time audit to assess how much time you currently spend with your family. Identify areas where you can reduce work-related activities to create more family time.

2. Create Family Rituals: Develop new family rituals or traditions that everyone can look forward to. These could be weekly game nights, monthly outings, or daily check-ins.

3. Tech-Free Family Time: Implement tech-free family time periods where everyone agrees to unplug from digital devices and engage in meaningful activities together.

Reflection Questions: Saying No without Guilt

1. Current Challenges: What specific situations make it difficult for you to say no, and what emotions do you experience when faced with these challenges?

2. Personal Priorities: What are your personal priorities, and how does saying yes to additional commitments impact them?

3. Past Experiences: Reflect on past experiences where you said no successfully. What positive outcomes resulted from setting those boundaries?

4. Self-Compassion: How can you practice self-compassion and remind yourself that it's okay to prioritize your own well-being?

5. Support Network: Who in your support network can help you reinforce your boundaries and provide encouragement when you need to say no?

Transformative Exercises:

1. Practice Saying No: Write down different scenarios where you might need to say no. Practice your responses, focusing on being honest, clear, and kind.

2. No Journal: Keep a "no journal" where you document instances when you said no. Reflect on how you felt before and after, and any positive outcomes that followed.

3. Visualize Success: Visualize scenarios where you need to say no and imagine yourself doing so confidently and without guilt. Use this visualization to build your confidence.

CHAPTER FIVE.
SELF-CARE ESSENTIALS.

WHY SELF-CARE IS NON-NEGOTIABLE.

When we hear the term "self-care," it's easy to picture a luxurious spa day, a long bubble bath, or perhaps a quiet evening with a good book. While these activities can certainly be part of self-care, the concept goes much deeper. At its core, self-care is about taking deliberate actions to maintain and improve your physical, mental, and emotional health. It's about making choices that replenish your energy, restore your well-being, and ensure you can meet the demands of your daily life.

Why is Self-Care Non-Negotiable?

In this achievement-oriented society, self-care often falls by the wayside. We prioritize work, family, and social obligations, frequently at the expense of our own health and happiness. However, neglecting self-care isn't sustainable. Without it, we risk burnout, chronic stress, and a host of physical and mental health issues. Here's why self-care must be a non-negotiable part of your life:

1. Sustaining Your Energy Levels:

Imagine your energy as a battery that needs regular recharging. Self-care activities are the charger that keeps you powered up. When you consistently neglect self-care, your battery runs down, leaving you feeling exhausted, overwhelmed, and unable to perform at your best. Regular self-care practices help maintain your energy levels, making you more resilient to stress and better equipped to handle life's challenges.

2. *Improving Physical Health:*

Self-care isn't just about mental and emotional well-being; it has a direct impact on your physical health too. Activities like regular exercise, healthy eating, and adequate sleep are fundamental aspects of self-care. They help boost your immune system, reduce the risk of chronic diseases, and improve your overall quality of life. Taking care of your body is essential for sustaining your long-term health and vitality.

3. *Enhancing Mental and Emotional Well-Being:*

Mental health is just as important as physical health. Self-care practices such as mindfulness, meditation, and spending time on hobbies can help reduce anxiety, improve mood, and enhance emotional resilience. When you take care of your mental and emotional health, you're better able to cope with stress, maintain healthy relationships, and enjoy a more balanced and fulfilling life.

4. *Fostering Self-Compassion:*

Self-care is an act of self-compassion. It's about recognizing your own worth and treating yourself with the same kindness and respect that you offer to others. When you prioritize self-care, you acknowledge that your needs and well-being are important. This fosters a healthier relationship with yourself, builds self-esteem, and promotes a more positive self-image.

5. Setting a Positive Example:

If you have children or others who look up to you, practicing self-care sets a positive example. It teaches them the importance of taking care of themselves and demonstrates that self-care is a vital part of a healthy, balanced life. By prioritizing your well-being, you can inspire those around you to do the same.

FINDING TIME FOR YOU: DAILY ROUTINES.

One of the biggest challenges to practicing self-care is finding the time. Between work, family, and other responsibilities, it can feel impossible to carve out even a few minutes for yourself. However, self-care doesn't have to be time-consuming. By incorporating small, manageable routines into your daily life, you can make self-care a seamless part of your day.

Finding Time for Self-Care.

Finding time for self-care can be challenging, but it's possible with some intentional planning and prioritization. Here are some strategies to help you find time for self-care:

1. Schedule It:

Treat self-care like any other important appointment by scheduling it into your calendar. Block out specific times for self-care activities and stick to them as you would any other commitment. Whether it's a morning workout, a midday walk, or an evening meditation session, scheduling self-care ensures that it becomes a regular part of your routine.

2. Start Small:

If you've never practiced self-care before, start with easy, gentle activities. Even just a few minutes of self-care each day can make a difference. As you become more comfortable with your self-care routine, you can gradually increase the time and complexity of your activities.

3. Combine Activities:

Look for opportunities to combine self-care with other daily activities. For example, listen to a guided meditation or an uplifting podcast while commuting, practice mindful eating during meals, or do gentle stretches while watching TV. Combining activities can help you incorporate self-care into your busy schedule without feeling overwhelmed.

4. Divide Responsibilities:

Delegate tasks and responsibilities to others without fear. Whether it's asking a family member to help with household chores or delegating tasks at work, sharing the load can free up time for self-care. Remember, taking care of yourself allows you to be more effective in all areas of your life.

5. *Make Self-Care Enjoyable:*

Choose self-care activities that you genuinely enjoy and look forward to. Whether it's a hobby, a creative pursuit, or a relaxing activity, finding joy in self-care makes it more sustainable. The more you enjoy your self-care routine, the more likely you are to stick with it.

Incorporating Self-Care into Your Life.

Self-care is an ongoing practice that evolves with your needs and circumstances. It's important to regularly assess your self-care routine and make adjustments as needed. Here are some pointers for introducing self-care into your life:

1. *Regular Self-Inspection:*

Set aside time for regular self-check-ins to assess how you're feeling and what you need. Consider journaling your thoughts and feelings, and use this reflection to identify areas where you may need more self-care. Regular check-ins can help you stay attuned to your well-being and make necessary adjustments to your routine.

2. *Flexibility and Adaptability:*

Life is unpredictable, and your self-care needs may change over time. Keep an adjustable and flexible self-care routine. If a certain activity no longer serves you, don't hesitate to try something new. The key is to stay open to evolving your self-care practices to meet your current needs.

3. Celebrate Small Wins:

Celebrate your self-care successes, no matter how small. Acknowledging and celebrating your efforts can boost your motivation and reinforce the importance of self-care. Whether it's completing a week of regular exercise or taking time for a relaxing bath, recognize and appreciate the positive steps you're taking.

4. Seek Assistance:

Don't be afraid to seek support from others. Whether it's talking to a friend, joining a self-care group, or seeking professional help, having a support system can make a big difference. Surround yourself with supportive people who can encourage and support your self-care journey.

5. Listen to Your Body:

Recognize your body's cues and attend to its needs. If you're feeling tired, rest. If you're feeling stressed, take a break. Listening to your body is a fundamental aspect of self-care and helps you stay in tune with your well-being.

Self-care is essential; it is neither a luxury nor an indulgence. It's about recognizing that you are worthy of care, love, and attention. By prioritizing self-care, you invest in your overall health and well-being, making you more resilient, happier, and better equipped to handle life's challenges.

PHYSICAL HEALTH: EXERCISE AND NUTRITION.

Why Physical Health Matters.

Your body is your most valuable asset. Taking care of it through regular exercise and proper nutrition is essential for maintaining energy levels, preventing chronic diseases, and promoting overall well-being. When you feel good physically, it positively impacts your mental and emotional health, enabling you to handle life's challenges more effectively.

The Benefits of Regular Exercise.

Exercise is a cornerstone of physical health. It offers a wide range of benefits, which include:

- ***Increased Energy Levels:*** Regular physical activity boosts your energy by improving cardiovascular health and enhancing the efficiency of your heart and lungs.
- ***Improved Mood:*** Exercise stimulates the production of endorphins, the body's natural mood lifters, which can help reduce stress, anxiety, and depression.

- **Better Sleep:** Engaging in physical activity helps regulate your sleep patterns, leading to deeper and more restful sleep.
- **Weight Management:** Exercise helps you maintain a healthy weight by burning calories and building muscle.
- **Disease Prevention:** Regular physical activity reduces the risk of chronic conditions such as heart disease, diabetes, and certain cancers.

Finding the Right Exercise for You.

The key to maintaining a consistent exercise routine is finding activities you enjoy. The following tips will help you determine what is most effective for you:

1. *Explore Different Activities*: Experiment with various types of exercise to see what you enjoy. This could include walking, running, swimming, cycling, yoga, weightlifting, or team sports.

2. *Start Small:* If you're new to exercise, start with small, manageable goals. Even a 10-minute walk each day can make a significant difference. As you get comfortable, gradually increase the timeframe and intensity.

3. *Make it Social:* Exercising with a friend or joining a group class can make physical activity more enjoyable and provide motivation and accountability.

4. *Schedule It In:* Treat exercise like any other important appointment by scheduling it into your calendar. In order to fully benefit from physical activity, consistency is key.

5. Pay attention to Your Body: Listen to how your body feels during and after exercise. If you experience pain or discomfort, adjust your routine accordingly and consult a healthcare professional if necessary.

Creating a Balanced Exercise Routine.

A well-rounded exercise routine should include a mix of cardiovascular, strength, flexibility, and balance exercises. Here's a simple guide to help you create a balanced routine:

1. Cardiovascular Exercise: Aim for at least 150 minutes of moderate-intensity or 75 minutes of high-intensity cardio each week. Exercises like brisk walking, jogging, cycling, or swimming are examples.

2. Strength Training: Include at least two days a week of strength training activities. This may include weightlifting, bodyweight exercises, or resistance band trainings. Strength training assists in building muscle, improve bone density, and boost metabolism.

3. Flexibility and Balance: Include flexibility and balance exercises in your routine to improve your range of motion and prevent injuries. Yoga, pilates, and stretching exercises are excellent options.

4. Rest and Recovery: Allow your body time to rest and recover between workouts. Overtraining can lead to injuries and burnout, so be sure to listen to your body and take rest days as needed.

Nutrition: Fueling Your Body

What you eat has a profound impact on your physical health, energy levels, and overall well-being. Proper nutrition provides your body with the essential nutrients it needs to function optimally, support immune function, and maintain a healthy weight.

Healthy Eating Habits.

Healthy eating habits is crucial for sustaining long-term health. Here are some essential tips to help you:

1. *Eat a Balanced Diet:* Aim for a balanced diet that includes a variety of foods from all food groups. This can include fruits, vegetables, whole grains, lean proteins, and good fats.

2. *Remain Hydrated*: To stay hydrated throughout the day, drink plenty of water. Digestion, nutrient absorption, and overall health all depend on water. Aim for at least eight glasses of water or more if you engage in physically activities daily.

3. *Adopt Portion Control:* Be mindful of serving sizes to avoid excessive consumption. Use smaller plates, pay attention to hunger and fullness cues, and avoid eating out of boredom or stress.

4. *Limit Processed Foods:* Minimize your intake of processed and sugary foods, as they can contribute to weight gain and various health issues. Eat diets high in whole, nutrient-dense foods that nourish your body.

5. *Plan and Prepare Meals:* Take the time to plan and prepare your meals in advance. This can help you make healthier choices and avoid the temptation of fast food or unhealthy snacks.

Nutrient-Dense Foods to Include in Your Diet

Incorporate the following nutrient-dense foods into your diet to support optimal health:

1. Fruits and Vegetables: Aim for a variety of colorful fruits and vegetables to ensure you get a wide range of vitamins, minerals, and antioxidants. Berries, leafy greens, carrots, and bell peppers are examples.

2. Whole Grains: Opt for whole grains such as brown rice, quinoa, oats, and whole wheat bread. These provide fiber, which aids in digestion and helps you feel full longer.

3. Lean Proteins: Include lean protein sources such as chicken, turkey, fish, beans, lentils, and tofu. Protein is essential for muscle repair and growth.

4. Healthy Fats: Incorporate healthy fats from sources like avocados, nuts, seeds, and olive oil. Healthy fats are crucial for brain functions and hormone production.

5. Dairy or Dairy Alternatives: Choose low-fat dairy options or fortified dairy alternatives such as almond milk or soy milk to ensure you get enough calcium and vitamin D.

MENTAL HEALTH: MINDFULNESS AND RELAXATION TECHNIQUES.

Just as physical health is crucial for overall well-being, so is mental health. How you think, feel, and act is influenced by your mental state. It also influences how you handle stress, relate to others, and make decisions. Prioritizing mental health through mindfulness and relaxation techniques can enhance your quality of life and help you manage the demands of work and daily life more effectively.

What is Mindfulness?

Mindfulness is the practice of being fully present and involved and judgement-free in the here and now. It involves paying attention to your thoughts, feelings, and physical sensations with an attitude of curiosity and acceptance. Mindfulness can be practiced through meditation, breathing exercises, and mindful movement.

Benefits of Mindfulness

Practicing mindfulness offers numerous benefits, including:

-**Reduced Stress:** Mindfulness helps reduce stress by encouraging a state of relaxation and promoting a sense of calm.

-**Improved Focus:** By training your mind to stay present, mindfulness enhances your ability to concentrate and stay focused on tasks.

-**Enhanced Emotional Regulation:** Mindfulness helps you become more aware of your emotions and respond to them in a balanced way.

-***Better Relationships:*** Practicing mindfulness can improve your communication and empathy, leading to stronger and more meaningful relationships.

How to Practice Mindfulness.

Incorporating mindfulness into your daily routine doesn't require a lot of time or special equipment.

Here are a few easy ways for practicing mindfulness:

1. Mindful Breathing: Take some time every day to concentrate on your breathing. Close your eyes, find a comfortable seat, and inhale deeply and slowly. Consider how your breath feels coming in and going out of your body.

2. Body Scan Meditation: This practice involves paying attention to different parts of your body, from head to toe. Lie down or sit comfortably and slowly bring your awareness to each part of your body, noticing any sensations or areas of tension.

3. Mindful Eating: Eat your meals slowly and attentively, savoring each bite. Take note of the taste, texture, and aroma of your food. Observe how your body feels prior to, during, and after eating.

4. Mindful Walking: Take a walk outside and focus on the sensation of your feet touching the ground, the movement of your body, and the sights and sounds around you. Walking mindfully can be a great way to connect with nature and clear your mind.

5. Mindfulness Apps: There are many apps available that offer guided mindfulness meditations and exercises. These can be helpful tools to incorporate mindfulness into your daily routine.

Relaxation Techniques: Finding Calm in the Chaos

In the world we live in today, taking time to relax is essential for maintaining mental health and overall well-being. Relaxation techniques help reduce stress, improve sleep, and enhance your ability to cope with life's challenges. Incorporating relaxation into your daily routine can provide a sense of balance and calm amid the chaos.

Relaxation Techniques to Try:

Here are some effective relaxation techniques to help you unwind and recharge:

1. Deep Breathing Exercises: Deep breathing is a simple yet powerful relaxation technique. Find a quiet place to sit or lie down, and take slow, deep breaths. Inhale deeply through your nose, hold for a few seconds, and exhale slowly through your mouth. Focus on the sensation of your breath and allow yourself to relax with each exhale.

2. Progressive Muscle Relaxation: This technique involves contracting and then relaxing various muscle groups in your body. Begin with your toes and work your way up to your head, tensing each muscle for a few seconds before relaxing.

This practice helps you become more aware of physical tension and promotes relaxation.

3. *Visualization:* Visualization involves imagining a peaceful and calming scene in your mind. Close your eyes and picture yourself in a serene environment, such as a beach, forest, or meadow. Engage all your senses by imagining the sights, sounds, smells, and sensations of this place. Visualization can help in relieve stress and increase sense of calm.

4. *Yoga:* Yoga combines physical postures, breathing exercises, and meditation to promote relaxation and reduce stress. Practicing yoga regularly can improve flexibility, strength, and mental clarity. There are many styles of yoga, so find one that suits your needs and preferences.

5. *Guided Meditation:* Guided meditation involves listening to a recorded meditation led by a teacher or guide. These meditations often include instructions for deep breathing, visualization, and mindfulness. Guided meditation can be a helpful tool for beginners and those looking to deepen their practice.

6. *Aromatherapy:* Aromatherapy uses essential oils to promote relaxation and well-being. Scents like lavender, chamomile, and eucalyptus are known for their calming effects. You can use essential oils in a diffuser, add them to a warm bath, or apply them to your skin (diluted with a carrier oil).

7. *Listening to Music:* Listening to calming music can help reduce stress and promote relaxation. Create a playlist of your favorite soothing tunes and take time to listen and unwind.

Creating a Relaxation Routine.

To reap the benefits of relaxation, it's important to make it a regular part of your routine. Here are some tips for incorporating relaxation into your daily life:

1. Set Aside Time: Schedule dedicated time for relaxation each day, even if it's just a few minutes. Consistency is key to making relaxation a habit.

2. Create a Relaxing Environment: Designate a space in your home where you can relax without distractions. This could be a cozy corner with a comfortable chair, soft lighting, and calming scents.

3. Combine Techniques: Experiment with different relaxation techniques and find what works best for you. You might find that a combination of deep breathing, visualization, and yoga is most effective.

4. Be Present: When practicing relaxation techniques, focus on being fully present in the moment. Let go of any worries or distractions and give yourself permission to relax.

5. Practice Self-Compassion: Be kind to yourself and acknowledge that relaxation is an important part of self-care. Allow yourself to take breaks and recharge without feeling guilty.

Conclusion

Self-care is an essential aspect of reclaiming your life from the demands of work. Taking care of yourself enables you to show up fully in all areas of your life, from your personal relationships to your professional responsibilities.

As you continue your journey toward reclaiming your life, keep these self-care essentials in mind. When you integrate regular exercise, proper nutrition, mindfulness, and relaxation techniques into your daily routine, you can support your overall well-being and find the balance you deserve.

By understanding the importance of self-care and implementing the strategies discussed in this chapter, you can create a robust self-care routine that supports your overall well-being. As you prioritize your physical and mental health, you'll find that you have more energy, focus, and resilience to navigate the demands of work and life. Remember, self-care is not selfish—it's an essential part of living a balanced and fulfilling life. Let's commit to taking care of ourselves and reclaiming our lives from the pressures of work.

Reflection Question: Why Self-Care is Non-Negotiable

What are the current stressors in your life, and how have they affected your physical and mental well-being?

Transformative Exercise: Write a letter to yourself describing why you deserve self-care. Highlight the importance of self-care in maintaining your overall health and how it benefits both your personal and professional life.

Reflection Question: Finding Time for You

How do you currently spend your time each day? Identify activities that consume your time but do not contribute to your well-being.

Transformative Exercise: Create a daily schedule that includes at least 30 minutes dedicated solely to self-care activities. This could include reading, taking a walk, meditating, or any other activity that helps you relax and recharge.

Reflection Question: Physical Health: Exercise and Nutrition

What are your current exercise and eating habits, and how do they impact your energy levels and overall health?

Transformative Exercise: Set specific, achievable goals for improving your physical health. For example, commit to a 15-minute walk each day or replacing one unhealthy snack with a nutritious alternative. Track your progress over a month and reflect on the changes you notice in your energy and mood.

Reflection Question: Mental Health: Mindfulness and Relaxation Techniques

How often do you feel overwhelmed or anxious, and what coping mechanisms do you currently use to manage these feelings?

Transformative Exercise: Practice a mindfulness or relaxation technique, such as deep breathing or meditation, for at least 10 minutes each day. Keep a journal to document your experiences, noting any changes in your stress levels and overall mental clarity.

Reflection Question: Integrating Self-Care into Daily Life

Reflection Question: What barriers or challenges do you face in prioritizing self-care, and how can you address them?

Transformative Exercise: Develop a personalized self-care plan that outlines specific activities you will incorporate into your daily routine. Include strategies for overcoming potential obstacles, such as setting boundaries with work or seeking support from loved ones. Review and adjust your plan regularly to ensure it remains effective and sustainable.

Self-Care Letter

Write a heartfelt letter to yourself about the importance of self-care. Include reasons why self-care is essential for your health and happiness. Revisit this letter whenever you feel overwhelmed or guilty about taking time for yourself.

CHAPTER SIX.
BUILDING A SUPPORT SYSTEM.

THE IMPORTANCE OF COMMUNITY.

In our journey to reclaim our lives from the overwhelming demands of work, one key element stands out: community. The saying "no man is an island" holds profound truth, especially in the hustle and bustle of modern life. Having a supportive network of people around you can make a world of difference in how you navigate life's challenges and celebrate its joys.

Why Community Matters.

Being part of a community offers emotional support, practical assistance, and a sense of belonging. When you have a group of people who understand you, share your values, and are there for you, it serves as a safety net, catching you when you fall and lifting you up when you succeed.

Here are a few reasons why community is important:

Emotional Support: When you're feeling stressed, overwhelmed, or simply need someone to talk to, having friends, family, and mentors who can lend an ear and offer encouragement is invaluable. They can provide different perspectives on your problems and help you see solutions you might not have considered.

Practical Assistance: Community can also mean having people who can help you with tangible needs. This could be anything from helping you move to a new home, watching your kids for a few hours, or even offering professional advice. These practical supports ease your burden and make life's logistical challenges more manageable.

Sense of Belonging: Humans are inherently social creatures. Having a sense of belonging helps thrive. Being part of a community gives you a sense of belonging, which boosts your self-esteem and overall happiness. It helps you understand that you're not alone in your struggles and that others share similar experiences.

Shared Resources: Communities often pool resources, be it knowledge, skills, or physical items. This sharing fosters a collaborative environment where everyone benefits. For example, joining a professional group can provide access to a wealth of industry knowledge and opportunities that you might not have discovered on your own.

FINDING YOUR TRIBE: FRIENDS AND MENTORS.

Building a support system begins with finding your tribe—those friends, colleagues, and mentors who resonate with you and support your journey. Here's how you can find and cultivate these essential relationships.

Friends: The Heart of Your Support System

Friends form the core of your support system. They are the people you can be yourself with, who know your quirks and love you anyway. But finding and nurturing meaningful friendships requires effort and intention.

Identify Your Values and Interests:

Start by identifying your core values and interests. What do you care deeply about? What activities bring you joy? Finding friends who share these values and interests can lead to deeper and more meaningful connections.

Join Clubs and Groups:

One of the best ways to meet like-minded people is to join clubs, groups, or organizations that align with your interests. This could be anything from a book club to a sports team, a professional association, or a volunteer group. These settings provide natural opportunities to connect with others.

Be Open and Approachable:

Building friendships requires you to be open and approachable. Smile, make eye contact, and initiate conversations. Genuinely engage others in conversation by asking questions and paying attention.

Invest Time and Effort:

Friendships don't happen overnight. They require time and effort to develop. Make a point to stay in touch with new acquaintances. Invite them for coffee, plan activities together, and be consistent in your efforts to nurture the relationship.

Be a Good Friend:

Remember, friendship is a two-way street. Be there for your friends, offer support when they need it, and celebrate their successes. Being a reliable and supportive friend encourages others to reciprocate.

Mentors: Guides on Your Journey

Mentors are individuals who have more experience in a particular area and can offer guidance, support, and wisdom. Having a mentor can significantly impact your personal and professional growth.

Identify Potential Mentors:

Look for people who have achieved what you aspire to and who exemplify the qualities you admire. They could be colleagues, leaders in your industry, or individuals in your community.

Reach Out:

Never hesitate to reach out to potential mentors. Introduce yourself, express your admiration for their work, and explain why you're seeking their guidance. Be respectful of their time and make your request clear and concise.

Be Clear About Your Goals:

When you establish a mentorship, be clear about your goals and what you hope to achieve from the relationship. This helps your mentor understand how they can best support you.

Be Open to Feedback: Mentors can provide valuable feedback that can help you grow. Be open to their suggestions and willing to make changes based on their advice. This openness will help you make the most of the mentorship relationship.

Stay Connected:

Continue to communicate with your mentor on a regular basis. Keep them updated on your progress and seek their advice when needed. Building a long-term relationship with your mentor can provide ongoing support and guidance.

Joining Communities and Networks

In addition to building friendships and finding mentors, joining communities and networks can expand your support system. Here are a few methods for getting involved:

1. **Professional Associations:** Join professional associations related to your field. These organizations often offer networking events, workshops, and resources that can support your growth and development.

2. **Interest Groups:** Join groups that align with your interests and hobbies. Whether it's a book club, sports team, or hobby group, these communities provide opportunities to connect with like-minded people and build friendships.

3. **Online Communities:** Online communities and forums can provide valuable support and connection, especially if you're looking for specific advice or resources. Participate in discussions, share your experiences, and seek support from the community.

4. Volunteering: Volunteering for a cause you care about can help you connect with others who share your values and passions. It also provides opportunities to give back to the community and make a positive impact.

5. Networking Events: Attend networking events and conferences to meet new people and expand your professional network. These events provide opportunities to connect with potential mentors, collaborators, and friends.

Maintaining Your Support System

Building a support system is an ongoing process. Here are some tips for maintaining and nurturing your support system:

1. Regular Communication: Stay in touch with your friends, mentors, and community members. Regular communication helps strengthen your relationships and ensures you stay connected.

2. Offer Support: Support is a two-way street. Be there for your friends and mentors when they need help. Offering your support strengthens your relationships and creates a sense of reciprocity.

3. Be Present: Be present and engaged when interacting with your support system. Show genuine interest in their lives and be there to listen and support them.

4. Celebrate Together: Celebrate successes and milestones together. Sharing in each other's joy creates positive experiences and strengthens your bond.

5. Adapt and Grow: As your life and needs change, your support system may also evolve. Be open to adapting and growing your support system to meet your changing needs.

LEANING ON FAMILY FOR SUPPORT.

Family can be an invaluable source of support as you navigate the challenges of balancing work and life. While every family dynamic is unique, the love and understanding that often come from family members can provide a strong foundation for emotional and practical support.

Understanding the Role of Family

Family members can offer a variety of support types: emotional, practical, and sometimes even financial. They are often the people who know you best, understand your history, and can offer unconditional love and encouragement. Leaning on family can help you feel grounded and supported as you work towards achieving a better balance in your life.

1. Communicating Your Needs:

One of the most crucial aspects of leaning on family for support is open and honest communication. It's important to let your family know what you're going through and how they can help.

Here are some suggestions for efficient communication with your family:

1. *Be Honest and Direct:* Share your struggles and the stress you're experiencing. Let your family know what specific support you need, whether it's a listening ear, help with chores, or simply understanding your need for some alone time.

2. *Express Gratitude:* Show appreciation for the support your family provides. A simple thank you can go a long way in strengthening your relationships and encouraging ongoing support.

3. *Set Boundaries:* While family support is invaluable, it's also important to set boundaries to ensure your needs are met without feeling overwhelmed or overburdened. Communicate your limits clearly and respectfully.

4. *Involve Them in Solutions:* Engage your family in finding solutions to your challenges. This could mean creating a shared family calendar to balance everyone's schedules or developing a plan to share household responsibilities.

2. Emotional Support:

Family members can offer a safe space to express your emotions and share your experiences. Here are some ways to leverage their emotional support:

1. *Confide in Them:* Share your feelings and experiences with family members you trust. Talking about your challenges can help lighten the emotional load and provide you with new perspectives.

2. Seek Encouragement: Let your family know when you need encouragement or reassurance. Their positive reinforcement can boost your confidence and motivation.

3. Create Traditions: Establish regular family traditions or activities that provide opportunities for connection and relaxation. This could be a weekly family dinner, game night, or weekend outing.

3. Practical Support:

Family members can also provide practical support to help you manage your workload and responsibilities more effectively:

1. Share Responsibilities: Delegate household chores and responsibilities among family members. This can free up time and reduce your stress, allowing you to focus on other areas of your life.

2. Childcare Assistance: If you have children, family members can help with childcare, whether it's babysitting, school pickups, or helping with homework. This support can provide you with much-needed breaks and time to focus on work or self-care.

3. Errand Running: Family members can assist with errands like grocery shopping, picking up prescriptions, or other tasks that can be time-consuming. This practical support can help you manage your time more effectively.

4. Financial Advice or Assistance: In some cases, family members may offer financial support or advice. While this isn't always applicable, it can be a significant help during tough times.

PROFESSIONAL HELP: WHEN AND HOW TO SEEK IT

While family support is invaluable, there are times when seeking professional help is necessary and beneficial. Professional help can come in many forms, including therapy, coaching, or consulting with experts in specific fields. Knowing when and how to seek professional help can be crucial in maintaining your well-being and achieving a balanced life.

Recognizing the Need for Professional Help:

It's important to recognize the signs that indicate you may need professional help. Here are some scenarios where seeking professional support might be beneficial:

1. *Persistent Stress or Anxiety:* If you experience ongoing stress or anxiety that affects your daily functioning and well-being, it may be time to seek help from a mental health professional.

2. *Difficulty Managing Work-Life Balance:* If you're struggling to find a balance between work and personal life despite trying various strategies, a coach or counselor can provide guidance and support.

3. *Relationship Issues:* If your relationships with family, friends, or colleagues are strained and you're unable to resolve conflicts on your own, a therapist can help you navigate these challenges.

4. *Need for Specialized Knowledge:* Sometimes, you may require specialized knowledge or skills to address specific challenges, such as financial planning, career development, or health and wellness. Consulting with experts in these fields can provide you with the tools and information you need.

Types of Professional Help.

There are various types of professional help available, each offering different forms of support:

1. Therapists and Counselors: These mental health professionals can help you address emotional and psychological challenges, develop coping strategies, and improve your overall well-being.

2. Life Coaches: Life coaches can assist you in setting and achieving personal and professional goals, improving time management, and enhancing your overall life satisfaction.

3. Career Coaches: Career coaches specialize in helping you navigate your career path, whether it's finding a new job, advancing in your current role, or transitioning to a different field.

4. Financial Advisors: Financial advisors can provide guidance on managing your finances, planning for the future, and making informed financial decisions.

5. Health and Wellness Experts: Nutritionists, fitness trainers, and other health professionals can help you develop a healthy lifestyle and address specific health concerns.

6. Consultants: Consultants can offer specialized knowledge and advice in areas such as business management, organizational development, and productivity improvement.

How to Seek Professional Help.

Once you've recognized the need for professional help, the next step is to seek out the right support. Here are some tips to help you get through the process:

1. Identify Your Needs: Determine what type of professional help you need based on your specific challenges and goals. This will help you find the right expert to assist you.

2. Research and Referrals: Start by researching professionals in your area or seeking referrals from friends, family, or colleagues. Look for professionals with the appropriate qualifications, experience, and a good reputation.

3. Check Credentials: Verify the credentials and qualifications of the professionals you're considering. Ensure they are licensed and certified in their respective fields.

4. Initial Consultation: Many professionals offer an initial consultation to discuss your needs and determine if they are a good fit for you. Use this opportunity to ask questions, understand their approach, and assess your comfort level with them.

5. Set Clear Goals: Before starting your sessions, set clear goals for what you hope to achieve. Communicate these goals to your chosen professional so they can tailor their support to your needs.

6. *Commit to the Process*: Seeking professional help requires commitment and active participation. Be open to feedback, willing to make changes, and dedicated to working towards your goals.

Maximizing the Benefits of Professional Help

To make the most of your professional support, consider the following tips:

1. *Be Open and Honest*: Share your thoughts, feelings, and challenges openly with your professional support. Honesty is crucial for them to understand your situation and provide effective guidance.

2. *Follow Through*: Implement the strategies and recommendations provided by your professional support. Consistency and follow-through are key to achieving positive outcomes.

3. *Regular Check-Ins*: Schedule regular check-ins with your professional support to track your progress, address any new challenges, and adjust your goals as needed.

4. *Practice Self-Reflection*: Reflect on your experiences and progress regularly. Self-reflection helps you gain insights into your journey and recognize areas for further improvement.

5. *Seek Additional Resources*: In addition to professional help, explore additional resources such as books, workshops, and online courses that can complement your growth and development.

Combining Family Support and Professional Help

For many, the ideal support system is a combination of family support and professional help. Family provides the emotional and practical support that is rooted in personal connection, while professionals offer specialized knowledge and guidance. Here are some tips for combining these sources of support effectively:

1. Integrate Support Systems: Communicate with both your family and your professional support about your goals and challenges. This integration ensures that everyone involved is aware of your needs and can provide cohesive support.

2. Balance Emotional and Practical Support: Use your family for emotional support and day-to-day practical assistance, while relying on professionals for specialized advice and strategies.

3. Encourage Family Involvement: When appropriate, involve your family in sessions with your professional support. This can provide them with insights into your challenges and help them understand how to support you better.

4. Create a Support Network: Build a network of support that includes both family members and professionals. This network can offer diverse perspectives and comprehensive assistance.

5. Maintain Boundaries: Ensure that you maintain healthy boundaries with both your family and professional support.

This balance allows you to receive the benefits of each without feeling overwhelmed or dependent.

Conclusion

Building a robust support system is a crucial step in reclaiming your life from the demands of work. By leaning on family for support and seeking professional help when needed, you create a foundation of strength, resilience, and guidance. This dual support system can provide you with the emotional, practical, and specialized assistance necessary to achieve a balanced and fulfilling life.

Remember, you don't have to navigate this journey alone. Embrace the support available to you, whether it's from family members who love and understand you or professionals who offer expert guidance. Together, these sources of support can help you overcome challenges, achieve your goals, and reclaim your life from the pressures of work. By building and nurturing your support system, you create a powerful network that empowers you to thrive and live a more balanced, joyful life.

Reflection Questions: The Importance of Community

1. How do you define community in your life?

Think about the groups of people that make you feel supported and understood. How do they contribute to your sense of belonging?

2. What qualities do you value most in a supportive community?

Identify the characteristics that are most important to you in a community, such as trust, empathy, or shared interests.

3. How do you currently contribute to your community?

Consider the ways in which you give back or support others within your community. How does this involvement enhance your sense of connection?

Transformative Exercises:

1. Community Mapping Exercise:

Create a visual map of your community, including different groups or individuals who provide support in various areas of your life (e.g., work, hobbies, neighborhood). Identify any gaps and think about how you might fill them.

2. Join a New Group:

Choose a community group or organization that aligns with your interests or values. Attend a meeting or event to explore how this new group can enhance your support network.

Reflection Questions: Finding Your Tribe: Friends and Mentors

1. Who are the key friends and mentors in your life?

List the people who provide you with emotional support, guidance, and inspiration. Reflect on how they have influenced your personal and professional growth.

2. What qualities do you look for in a friend or mentor?

Consider the traits that are important to you, such as trustworthiness, empathy, experience, or shared values.

3. How have your friends and mentors supported you during challenging times?

Recall specific instances where their support made a significant difference in your life. How did their involvement help you navigate those challenges?

4. How do you support your friends and mentors in return?

Reflect on the ways you contribute to these relationships. How do you show appreciation, provide support, and maintain these connections?

Transformative Exercises:

1. Network Expansion Plan:

Create a plan to expand your network by identifying specific groups, events, or individuals you want to connect with. Set realistic goals for reaching out and building new relationships.

2. Mentorship Request:

Identify a potential mentor in your field or area of interest. Reach out to them with a thoughtful request for mentorship, explaining why you admire their work and how you hope they can guide you.

3. Support Exchange:

Arrange a mutual support exchange with a friend or mentor. Offer your skills or assistance in an area they need help with, and ask for their support in return. This exercise fosters reciprocity and deeper connections.

4. *Gratitude Letters:*

Write letters of gratitude to your friends and mentors, expressing your appreciation for their support and influence. Deliver these letters in person or through a heartfelt email, and notice the positive impact it has on your relationships.

Reflection Questions: Leaning on Family for Support

1. How has your family supported you in the past?

Reflect on specific instances where family members provided emotional, practical, or financial support. How did their involvement help you?

2. What challenges have you faced in communicating your needs to your family?

Consider any difficulties you've experienced in expressing your needs and seeking support from family members. How can you improve this communication?

3. What boundaries do you need to set with your family to ensure a healthy support system?

Identify any areas where you need to establish boundaries to maintain a balanced and healthy relationship with your family.

4. How can you show appreciation for your family's support?

Reflect on ways to express gratitude and appreciation for the support your family provides. How can you strengthen these bonds through acknowledgment and reciprocation?

Transformative Exercises:

1. Family Meeting:

Organize a family meeting to discuss your work-life balance goals and the support you need. Use this time to communicate your needs, set boundaries, and develop a plan for mutual support.

2. Shared Activities:

Plan a regular family activity that provides an opportunity for bonding and relaxation. This could be a weekly game night, a monthly outing, or a daily walk together.

Reflection Questions: Professional Help: When and How to Seek It

1. What signs indicate that you might need professional help?

Reflect on any persistent challenges or symptoms that suggest you could benefit from professional support. How do these issues impact your daily life and well-being?

2. What type of professional help do you need?

Consider the specific areas where you need support, such as mental health, career development, financial planning, or health and wellness. What kind of professional can best address these needs?

3. How do you feel about getting professional assistance?

Reflect on any reservations or fears you have about seeking professional support. What beliefs or experiences contribute to these feelings?

4. What are the benefits of seeking professional help?

Consider the potential positive outcomes of engaging with a professional. How can their expertise and guidance help you achieve your goals and improve your well-being?

Transformative Exercises:

1. Research and Shortlist:

Research different professionals in your area or field of interest, such as therapists, coaches, or consultants. Create a shortlist of potential candidates and note their qualifications, experience, and reviews.

2. Initial Consultation:

Schedule an initial consultation with a professional from your shortlist. Use this meeting to discuss your needs, ask questions, and assess whether they are a good fit for you.

3. Professional Support Journal:

Keep a journal to document your experiences and progress when working with a professional. Reflect on the insights gained, strategies learned, and any changes in your well-being.

4. Commitment Contract:

Write a commitment contract with yourself to actively engage in the process of seeking professional help. Outline your goals, the steps you will take, and a timeline for seeking support.

CHAPTER SEVEN.
FLEXIBILITY AT WORK.

In our modern world, flexibility at work has become a crucial factor in maintaining a healthy work-life balance. As we navigate through different job roles and personal commitments, the ability to adapt and manage our work environment can significantly enhance our well-being and productivity. In this chapter, we'll explore how to make the most of remote work and effectively negotiate for better work conditions. These strategies will help you create a more flexible, balanced, and fulfilling work life.

REMOTE WORK: TIPS AND TRICKS.

Remote work, once a novelty, has now become a staple for many of us. Whether you're working from home full-time or adopting a hybrid model, mastering remote work can lead to greater flexibility and efficiency. Here are some tips and tricks to help you thrive in a remote work environment.

1. Create a Dedicated Workspace:

One of the biggest challenges of remote work is separating your work life from your personal life. Creating a dedicated workspace can help you establish boundaries and maintain focus.

- **Choose the Right Spot:** Find a quiet, well-lit area in your home where you can work without distractions. Ideally, this should be a space you can leave at the end of the workday to mentally 'clock out.'
- **Ergonomics Matter:** Invest in a comfortable chair and a proper desk setup. Your physical comfort can greatly impact your productivity and health.
- **Personalize Your Space:** Make your workspace inviting and inspiring. Make it a space you love being in by adding some personal touches, such as pictures, plants, or artwork.

2. Establish a Routine:

Having a consistent routine can help you stay organized and focused, even when working remotely.

- **Set Regular Hours:** Try to start and end your workday at the same time each day. This consistency can help you maintain a work-life balance.
- **Morning Rituals:** Begin your day with a routine that prepares you for work. This could include a morning workout, meditation, or a cup of coffee while reviewing your day's tasks.
- **Take Breaks:** Schedule regular breaks to stretch, walk around, and recharge. Taking short breaks might increase productivity and help you avoid burnout.

3. Communicate Effectively:

A successful remote work requires regular and transparent communication. Keeping in touch with your team and manager can prevent misunderstandings and foster collaboration.

- **Use the Right Tools:** Make use of communication tools like Slack, Microsoft Teams, or Zoom to stay connected. Choose the platform that works best for your team and stick with it.
- **Regular Check-ins:** Schedule regular check-ins with your manager and team to discuss progress, challenges, and upcoming tasks. These meetings can help keep everyone on the same page.
- **Be Proactive:** Do not wait for others to reach out to you. If you need help or have questions, communicate proactively to keep things moving smoothly.

4. Stay Organized:

Staying organized is crucial for remote work. With the right tools and strategies, you can manage your tasks and responsibilities efficiently.

- **Task Management Tools:** Use tools like Trello, Asana, or Monday.com to keep track of your tasks and deadlines. These platforms can help you prioritize your work and collaborate with your team.
- **Time Management Techniques:** Techniques like the Pomodoro Technique (discussed in the previous chapter) can help you manage your time effectively and stay focused on your tasks.

- ***Declutter Regularly:*** A cluttered workspace can lead to a cluttered mind. Take a few minutes each day to tidy up your workspace and organize your materials.

5. Maintain Work-Life Balance:

Remote work has the potential to blur the lines between your business and personal lives. To avoid burnout, keep a good balance.

- ***Set Boundaries:*** Establish clear boundaries between your work and personal life. To avoid disruptions and distractions, communicate these boundaries to your family or housemates.
- ***Unplug After Work:*** Once your workday is over, make a conscious effort to unplug. Turn off work notifications and focus on personal activities or hobbies.
- ***Prioritize Self-Care:*** Make time for self-care activities that help you relax and recharge. This could include activities such as exercise, reading, or spending time with your loved ones.

NEGOTIATING FOR BETTER WORK CONDITIONS.

Negotiating for better work conditions is essential for creating a flexible and supportive work environment. Whether you're looking to adjust your work hours, increase your remote work days, or improve your overall working conditions, effective negotiation skills can help you achieve your goals.

1. Know Your Needs and Priorities:

Before entering any negotiation, it's important to clearly understand your needs and priorities. Reflect on what changes would most improve your work-life balance and job satisfaction.

- ***Identify Key Areas:*** Consider aspects like flexible hours, remote work options, professional development opportunities, and work environment improvements.
- ***Rank Your Priorities:*** Determine which areas are most important to you and which ones you're willing to compromise on. This clarity will enable you to negotiate more efficiently.

2. Research and Prepare:

Preparation is key to successful negotiation. Gather information and data to support your requests and demonstrate the benefits of the proposed changes.

- ***Research Industry Standards:*** Look into what other companies in your industry are offering. This can provide a benchmark and strengthen your case.
- ***Document Your Achievements:*** Compile evidence of your contributions and achievements. Identify how your performance has positively impacted the company.

- ***Anticipate Objections:*** Think about potential objections your employer might have and prepare counterarguments. This preparation will help you address concerns confidently.

3. Build a Strong Case:

Presenting a compelling case for your desired work conditions involves framing your requests in a way that highlights mutual benefits for both you and your employer.

- ***Focus on Benefits:*** Emphasize how the proposed changes will benefit the company, such as increased productivity, reduced absenteeism, or improved employee morale.
- ***Provide Data:*** Use data and examples to support your case. For instance, if you're requesting flexible hours, present studies showing how flexible work arrangements can boost productivity.
- ***Highlight Your Value:*** Remind your employer of your contributions and the value you bring to the organization. Acknowledge your commitment to maintaining high performance under the new conditions.

4. Choose the Right Time and Approach:

Timing and approach can have a great influence the outcome of your negotiation. Choose a moment when your employer is likely to be receptive and approach the conversation professionally.

- **Schedule a Meeting:** Request a dedicated meeting to discuss your work conditions. This shows that you're serious and allows for a focused conversation.
- **Be Professional:** Approach the negotiation with a positive and professional attitude. Avoid making demands and instead present your requests as mutually beneficial proposals.
- **Stay Calm and Composed:** Negotiations can be stressful, but it's important to remain calm and composed. Listen actively, respond thoughtfully, and maintain a respectful tone.

5. Be Open to Compromise:

Negotiation often involves finding a middle ground. Be open to compromise and willing to adjust your requests to reach a mutually satisfactory agreement.

- **Prioritize Flexibility:** While it's important to advocate for your needs, be flexible and willing to consider alternative solutions. Your employer may have constraints that require compromise.
- **Explore Win-Win Solutions:** Look for solutions that benefit both you and your employer. For example, if full-time remote work isn't feasible, propose a hybrid model that balances office and remote work.
- **Stay Positive:** Maintain a positive attitude throughout the negotiation process. Even if you don't get everything you asked for, demonstrating flexibility and cooperation can lead to future opportunities for negotiation.

6. Follow Up and Evaluate:

After reaching an agreement, it's important to follow up and evaluate the effectiveness of the new work conditions. Regular check-ins can help ensure that both parties are satisfied and address any issues that arise.

- ***Set Clear Expectations:*** Make sure that both you and your employer have a clear understanding of the agreed-upon changes. Document the terms in writing if necessary.
- ***Regular Check-Ins:*** Schedule regular check-ins with your manager to discuss how the new work conditions are working out. Use these meetings to provide feedback and address any concerns.
- ***Evaluate and Adjust:*** Continuously evaluate the effectiveness of the new work conditions. If adjustments are needed, approach your employer with constructive feedback and suggestions for improvement.

Combining Remote Work and Negotiation Skills.

To create the most flexible and supportive work environment, consider combining the tips and tricks for remote work with your negotiation skills. By doing so, you can enhance your remote work experience and secure better work conditions that support your overall well-being.

1. Advocate for Remote Work Options:

If you're not currently working remotely or want to increase your remote work days, use your negotiation skills to advocate for this change. Present the benefits of remote work for both you and the company, and provide data to support your case.

- ***Highlight Productivity Gains:*** Emphasize how remote work can lead to increased productivity, reduced commuting time, and lower stress levels.
- ***Showcase Success Stories:*** Share examples of other companies or teams that have successfully implemented remote work arrangements. Highlight the positive outcomes they've experienced.
- ***Propose a Trial Period:*** If your employer is hesitant, propose a trial period for remote work. This allows both parties to evaluate the arrangement and make adjustments as needed.

2. Negotiate Flexible Hours:

Flexible hours can greatly enhance your work-life balance by allowing you to work during your most productive times and accommodate personal commitments. Use your negotiation skills to request flexible hours that align with your needs.

- ***Present the Benefits:*** Explain how flexible hours can improve your productivity, reduce burnout, and enhance your overall job satisfaction.
- ***Offer Solutions:*** Propose specific solutions, such as a flexible start and end time, compressed workweeks, or staggered hours. Be prepared to discuss how these

changes can be implemented without disrupting business operations.
- **Provide a Plan:** Present a detailed plan for how you will manage your workload and stay connected with your team while working flexible hours.

3. Enhance Your Remote Work Environment:

If you're already working remotely, use your negotiation skills to enhance your remote work environment. This could involve requesting better tools, technology, or support to improve your productivity and comfort while working from home.

- **Request Necessary Equipment:** If you need specific equipment or technology to enhance your remote work setup, present a case for why these items are essential. This might include ergonomic furniture, upgraded computer hardware, or software subscriptions.
- **Propose Training Opportunities:** Suggest professional development opportunities that can help you and your team work more effectively in a remote environment. This might include training on collaboration tools, time management, or remote leadership.
- **Seek Support Resources:** If you're struggling with aspects of remote work, such as isolation or work-life boundaries, request access to support resources. This could include virtual wellness programs, counseling services, or peer support groups.

4. Foster a Remote Work Culture:

Building a supportive remote work culture can enhance your overall experience and improve team cohesion. Use your negotiation skills to advocate for initiatives that foster a positive remote work environment.

- ***Encourage Regular Communication:*** Propose regular virtual team meetings, check-ins, and social events to maintain strong communication and team spirit.
- ***Promote Flexibility:*** Advocate for a culture that values flexibility and trusts employees to manage their time effectively. This can include flexible hours, asynchronous communication, and a results-oriented approach.
- ***Support Mental Health:*** Suggest initiatives that support mental health and well-being, such as virtual mindfulness sessions, wellness challenges, or mental health days.

Real-Life Examples of Successful Remote Work and Negotiation.

To illustrate the effectiveness of these strategies, let's explore a few real-life examples of individuals who have successfully negotiated better remote work conditions:

1. Lilian's Flexible Hours.

Lilian, a marketing manager, found that her productivity peaked in the early morning and late afternoon. She negotiated with her employer to adjust her work hours, allowing her to start and finish earlier than the traditional 9-to-5 schedule. By presenting data on her productivity patterns and highlighting how the change would benefit her work-life balance, Lilian secured flexible hours that enhanced her performance and well-being.

2. James' Remote Work Setup.

James, a software developer, struggled with back pain due to his home office setup. He presented a case to his employer for ergonomic furniture, including a standing desk and an ergonomic chair. By emphasizing the health benefits and potential for increased productivity, James successfully negotiated for the necessary equipment to create a comfortable and efficient remote work environment.

3. Emma's Professional Development.

Emma, a project manager, recognized the need for better remote collaboration skills within her team. She proposed a series of virtual training sessions on tools like Slack and Asana, highlighting how these sessions could improve team communication and project management. Her employer agreed, and the training sessions led to smoother remote operations and enhanced team cohesion.

4. Carlos' Mental Health Support.

Carlos, a customer service representative, experienced stress and burnout while working remotely. He requested access to virtual counseling services and wellness programs offered by the company. By demonstrating the link between mental health support and employee productivity, Carlos successfully negotiated for these resources, improving his well-being and job satisfaction.

Practical Tips for Implementing Remote Work and Negotiation Skills

Here are some practical tips to help you implement remote work strategies and enhance your negotiation skills:

1. Document Your Achievements:

Keep a record of your achievements, feedback from colleagues, and performance metrics. This documentation can serve as evidence to support your negotiation requests.

2. Stay Informed:

Stay informed about industry trends, best practices, and company policies related to remote work. This knowledge can help you build a stronger case during negotiations.

3. Seek Feedback:

Regularly seek feedback from your manager and colleagues on your remote work performance. Use this feedback to identify areas for improvement and to strengthen your negotiation arguments.

4. Develop Soft Skills:

Develop soft skills such as communication, adaptability, and problem-solving. These skills are crucial for both remote work and successful negotiation.

5. Join Professional Networks:

Join professional networks and online communities related to remote work and negotiation. These networks can provide valuable insights, resources, and support.

Conclusion.

Creating a flexible and supportive work environment is essential for maintaining a healthy work-life balance and achieving long-term career success. By mastering remote work techniques and honing your negotiation skills, you can take control of your work environment and create conditions that support your well-being and productivity. Remember, flexibility is not just about adapting to change but also about actively shaping your work life to meet your needs and goals. With the right strategies and a proactive approach, you can reclaim your life from work and enjoy a more balanced, fulfilling career.

JOB CRAFTING – MAKING YOUR JOB WORK FOR YOU.

In today's ever-evolving work environment, the concept of job crafting has emerged as a powerful tool for enhancing job satisfaction, productivity, and overall well-being. Job crafting is about taking proactive steps to redesign your job in ways that better align with your skills, interests, and values. It allows you to mold your role to fit your strengths and passions, thereby making your job more enjoyable and fulfilling. Let's dive into how you can start job crafting to make your job work for you.

Understanding Job Crafting.

Job crafting involves taking intentional actions to shape and customize your job. It's about making small, strategic changes to your tasks, relationships, and perceptions at work to create a more meaningful and satisfying job experience. Job crafting can be broken down into three main types:

1. *Task Crafting:* Altering the scope, sequence, or nature of your tasks.

2. *Relational Crafting:* Changing the nature or extent of your interactions with others.

3. *Cognitive Crafting:* Changing how you perceive your job to find more meaning in what you do.

By engaging in job crafting, you can transform your job into one that not only meets your professional needs but also nurtures your personal growth and happiness.

Task Crafting: Shaping Your Responsibilities.

Task crafting involves modifying your job responsibilities to better suit your strengths and interests. Here's how you can start task crafting:

Identify Core and Peripheral Tasks:

Begin by listing all the tasks you perform in your job. Separate them into core tasks (essential duties) and peripheral tasks (additional responsibilities). Identify which tasks energize you and which ones drain you.

- ***Enhance Enjoyable Tasks:*** Look for ways to increase the time you spend on tasks that you enjoy and are good at. For example, if you love creating presentations, volunteer to handle more of them.

- ***Minimize Draining Tasks:*** Find ways to reduce, delegate, or streamline tasks that drain your energy. If possible, propose process improvements or automation for these tasks.

Introduce New Tasks:

Consider introducing new tasks that align with your interests and career goals. This could involve proposing projects or initiatives that leverage your unique skills.

- ***Propose Projects:*** Suggest projects that you are passionate about and that add value to your team or organization. For instance, if you're passionate about sustainability, propose a green initiative.

- ***Seek Skill Development Opportunities:*** Volunteer for tasks that help you develop new skills or expand your expertise. This not only enriches your job but also enhances your career prospects.

Reframe Existing Tasks:

Sometimes, simply changing the way you approach or think about your tasks can make a significant difference.

- ***Find Meaning:*** Reflect on how your tasks contribute to the larger goals of your organization. Understanding the impact of your work can increase your sense of purpose and motivation.

- ***Innovate:*** Look for creative ways to approach routine tasks. Experimenting with new methods or tools can make your work more interesting and efficient.

Relational Crafting: Enhancing Work Relationships

Relational crafting involves modifying your interactions with colleagues, clients, and others to improve your work experience.

Here are a few tips on how to do this:

1. Build Positive Relationships:

Strong, positive relationships at work can enhance your job satisfaction and performance. Concentrate on establishing and nurturing these connections.

- **Network Actively:** Take the initiative to connect with colleagues across different departments. Networking can create opportunities for collaboration and assistance.

- **Mentorship:** Find mentors who can offer guidance and help. Additionally, consider mentoring others, which can be rewarding and help you build strong relationships.

2. Manage Negative Interaction:

Negative interactions can significantly impact your well-being. Find ways to manage or minimize these interactions.

- **Set Boundaries:** Politely but firmly set boundaries with colleagues who create stress or negativity. This can involve limiting unnecessary interactions or addressing issues directly.

- **Seek Resolution:** If conflicts arise, seek to resolve them constructively. Open communication and problem-solving can improve relationships and create a more positive work environment.

3. Collaborate Effectively:

Effective collaboration can enhance your job satisfaction and lead to better outcomes for your team.

- **Communicate Clearly:** Clear, open communication is key to successful collaboration. Share your ideas, listen actively, and provide constructive feedback.

- **_Leverage Strengths:_** Recognize and leverage the strengths of your colleagues. Working together can create a more dynamic and productive team environment.

Cognitive Crafting: Changing Your Perspective

Cognitive crafting involves changing how you perceive your job to make it more meaningful and satisfying.

Here's how to do this:

1. Reflect on Your Work's Impact:

Take time to reflect on how your work contributes to the organization and society.

- **_Connect to the Bigger Picture:_** Understand how your role fits into the broader mission and goals of your organization. This can enhance your sense of purpose and motivation.

- **_Celebrate Wins:_** Acknowledge and celebrate your wins, both big and small. Recognizing your contributions can boost your morale and job satisfaction.

2. Focus on Growth and Learning:

Approach your job with a mindset focused on growth and learning.

- **Embrace Challenges:** See challenges as challenges for growth and progress. Embracing difficult tasks can help you develop new skills and gain confidence.

- **Seek Feedback:** Regularly seek feedback from colleagues and supervisors. Constructive feedback can help you improve and advance in your career.

3. Practice Gratitude:

Gratitude can significantly enhance your job satisfaction and overall well-being.

- **Keep a Gratitude Journal:** Regularly write down things you are grateful for at work. This practice can shift your focus from negative aspects to positive ones.

- **Express Appreciation:** Take the time to thank colleagues and acknowledge their contributions. Expressing gratitude can strengthen relationships and create a positive work environment.

Real-Life Examples of Job Crafting

To illustrate the impact of job crafting, let's look at a few real-life examples:

Example 1: Task Crafting for Innovation

Maria, a product manager, felt that her job was becoming monotonous. She enjoyed brainstorming and creative thinking but spent most of her time on routine administrative tasks. Maria proposed a new initiative to develop innovative product ideas, allowing her to engage in creative tasks while still fulfilling her core responsibilities. This not only revitalized her interest in her job but also led to the development of successful new products.

Example 2: Relational Crafting for Support

John, an IT specialist, found his job isolating as he worked mostly independently. He decided to build stronger relationships with his colleagues by organizing regular lunch meetings and after-work activities. This helped him feel more connected and supported, enhancing his job satisfaction and sense of belonging.

Example 3: Cognitive Crafting for Purpose

Emma, a customer service representative, struggled with the repetitive nature of her job. She started to focus on how her role helped customers and the positive impact she had on their lives. By reframing her perspective, Emma found greater meaning and fulfillment in her work, which improved her performance and satisfaction.

Practical Steps to Start Job Crafting

Ready to start job crafting? Here are some practical methods to help you:

Step 1: Self-Assessment

Begin by assessing your current job and identifying areas for improvement.

1. ***List Your Tasks:*** Make a detailed list of your daily tasks and responsibilities.
2. ***Identify Strengths and Interests:*** Reflect on your strengths, interests, and values. Identify tasks that align with these aspects.
3. ***Evaluate Job Satisfaction:*** Assess your current level of job satisfaction and pinpoint areas where you feel unfulfilled or stressed.

Step 2: Set Goals

Set clear, achievable goals for your job crafting efforts.

1. ***Define Objectives:*** Determine what you want to achieve through job crafting. This could be increased job satisfaction, better work-life balance, or professional growth.
2. ***Create a Plan:*** Create a step-by-step plan to reach your goals. Outline specific actions you will take to modify your tasks, relationships, and perspectives.

Step 3: Take Action

Start implementing your job crafting plan.

1. **Modify Tasks:** Begin making changes to your tasks. Introduce new tasks, delegate less enjoyable ones, and reframe existing tasks to find more meaning.
2. **Enhance Relationships:** Focus on building positive relationships and managing negative interactions. Seek out collaboration opportunities and support networks.
3. **Shift Perspectives:** Practice cognitive crafting techniques such as reflecting on your work's impact, embracing challenges, and practicing gratitude.

Step 4: Monitor and Adjust

Regularly evaluate the impact of your job crafting efforts and make adjustments as needed.

1. **Seek Feedback:** Gather feedback from colleagues, supervisors, and mentors. Use this feedback to refine your job crafting strategies.
2. **Reflect on Progress:** Review your progress and accomplishments on a regular basis. Assess whether your job satisfaction and well-being have improved.
3. **Adjust Strategies:** Be flexible and willing to adjust your job crafting plan based on your experiences and changing circumstances.

Conclusion

Job crafting is a powerful tool for creating a more flexible, fulfilling, and meaningful work experience. By taking proactive steps to modify your tasks, relationships, and perspectives, you can transform your job to better align with your strengths and passions. Remember, job crafting is an ongoing process that requires self-awareness, creativity, and a willingness to adapt. With the right approach, you can make your job work for you and reclaim your life from work.

Reflection Questions

1. Remote Work: Tips and Tricks:

- How do you currently manage your time and tasks while working remotely? What strategies have you found most effective, and where do you struggle?

- What are the biggest challenges you face in maintaining work-life balance while working from home? How do you think you can navigate these challenges?

2. Negotiating for Better Work Conditions:

- What aspects of your current work conditions would you like to improve? How have you approached negotiations with your employer in the past?

- How do you feel about advocating for your needs at work? What fears or reservations do you have about negotiating for better work conditions?

3. Job Crafting: Making Your Job Work for You

- Which tasks in your job bring you the most satisfaction and which do you find draining? How can you reshape your responsibilities to better align with your strengths and interests?

- How can you improve your relationships with colleagues to enhance your job satisfaction? What steps can you take to foster a more supportive and collaborative work environment?

Transformative Exercises

1. Remote Work: Tips and Tricks:

- **Create a Personalized Remote Work Schedule:** Design a daily schedule that balances work and personal life. Include time blocks for focused work, breaks, exercise, and leisure activities. Test your schedule for a week and adjust based on what works best for you.

- **Set up an Ideal Workspace:** Evaluate your current remote work setup. Identify ways to improve your workspace to increase productivity and comfort, such as ergonomic furniture, proper lighting, and minimizing distractions.

2. Negotiating for Better Work Conditions:

- ***Develop a Negotiation Plan:*** Identify one aspect of your work conditions you want to improve (e.g., flexible hours, remote work options, better tools). Prepare a clear and concise proposal outlining the benefits to both you and your employer. Practice presenting your proposal to a friend or mentor for feedback.

   - ***Role-Playing Exercise:*** Partner with a colleague or friend to role-play a negotiation scenario. Take turns being the employee and the employer. This exercise will help you build confidence and refine your negotiation skills.

3. Job Crafting: Making Your Job Work for You:

   - ***Task Analysis and Reframing:*** List all your job tasks and categorize them into three groups: tasks you enjoy, tasks you find neutral, and tasks you dislike. For tasks you dislike, brainstorm ways to reframe or modify them to make them more engaging. For example, if you dislike routine reporting, think about how you can automate parts of the process or find new ways to present the data that might be more interesting.

   - ***Relationship Building Exercise:*** Identify three colleagues you would like to build stronger relationships with. Plan and initiate a coffee chat or virtual meeting with each person to discuss mutual interests, work challenges, and potential collaboration opportunities. Reflect on how these interactions impact your work experience and satisfaction.

CHAPTER EIGHT.
CULTIVATING HOBBIES AND INTERESTS.

Rediscovering Old Passions.

Remember that exhilarating feeling when you used to play the guitar, paint, or bake intricate pastries just for the fun of it? Life's responsibilities, especially work, often push these cherished activities to the back burner. But these hobbies, these passions, are a vital part of who you are. They breathe life into your routine, provide an escape from stress, and remind you of your true self beyond your professional identity.

The Power of Nostalgia.

Nostalgia isn't just a pleasant trip down memory lane; it can be a powerful motivator. Think about the hobbies you loved in your youth or early adulthood. Was it playing a sport, creating art, or exploring nature? Reconnecting with these activities can rekindle joy and creativity, offering a refreshing break from daily stressors. Plus, returning to a beloved hobby can evoke a sense of accomplishment and satisfaction that might be missing from your current routine.

Taking the First Steps.

The idea of getting back into an old hobby might seem daunting, especially if it's been a while. Start small. If you loved painting, begin with a simple sketch or an adult coloring book. If you were into music, pick up your instrument and play a favorite song. The goal is to reintroduce yourself to the activity without the pressure of mastering it immediately.

Making Time for Old Passions.

Finding time for hobbies in a busy schedule can be challenging, but it's crucial. Start by setting aside a specific time each week dedicated solely to your hobby. It could be an hour on a Sunday morning or a half-hour before bed. The key is consistency. Over time, this regular practice can become a cherished part of your routine, providing a much-needed break and a sense of personal fulfillment.

Sharing Your Passion.

Rediscovering an old hobby can be even more enjoyable when shared with others. Look for local clubs or online communities where you can connect with people who share your interests. Sharing your passion with others can provide motivation, inspiration, and a sense of camaraderie. Whether it's a knitting circle, a book club, or a hiking group, being part of a community can enhance your experience and keep you engaged.

Trying New Things: Expanding Your Horizons

While reconnecting with old hobbies is fulfilling, trying new things can be equally invigorating. Stepping out of your comfort zone and exploring new activities can open up a world of possibilities and help you discover new passions you never knew you had.

Embracing the Unknown.

Trying something new can be intimidating, but it's also an opportunity for growth. It's about giving yourself permission to be a beginner, to make mistakes, and to learn. Whether it's taking up a new sport, learning a new language, or trying a new craft, embracing the unknown can be a thrilling adventure.

Exploring Different Avenues.

The first step in trying something new is identifying what piques your interest. Think about activities you've always been curious about. Maybe you've always wanted to try pottery, salsa dancing, or coding. Make a list of these interests and choose one to start with. Remember, it's not about being perfect; it's about exploring and enjoying the process.

Finding Resources and Support.

There are countless resources available to help you get started with a new hobby. Online platforms offer tutorials and classes on virtually anything you can think of. Community centers, local colleges, and hobby stores often offer classes as well. Don't hesitate to reach out to friends or family members who might share your new interest. Their support and enthusiasm can make the experience even more enjoyable.

Balancing Old and New.

Balancing old hobbies with new interests can be a fun and rewarding challenge. It allows you to enjoy the comfort of familiar activities while experiencing the excitement of new ones. Schedule time for both in your routine, ensuring that you have a diverse range of activities that keep you engaged and fulfilled.

The Benefits of Hobbies and Interests.

Cultivating hobbies and interests goes beyond just filling time. These activities have profound benefits for your mental, emotional, and even physical well-being.

Here are a few benefits of hobbies and interests:

1. Reducing Stress and Anxiety:

Engaging in hobbies is a great way to reduce stress and anxiety. These activities divert your mind from everyday pressures and allow you to immerse yourself in something enjoyable. Whether it's gardening, playing a musical instrument, or knitting, the repetitive nature of many hobbies can be particularly soothing, helping to calm your mind and reduce stress levels.

2. Boosting Creativity:

Hobbies often require creative thinking and problem-solving, which can enhance your creativity in other areas of your life, including your work. Engaging in creative activities stimulates your brain, encouraging innovative thinking and a fresh perspective.

3. Improving Physical Health:

Many hobbies involve physical activity, which is beneficial for your health. Whether it's hiking, dancing, or playing a sport, physical hobbies help you stay active and improve your fitness. Even less strenuous activities like gardening or yoga can provide significant physical benefits.

4. Enhancing Social Connections:

Hobbies can also improve your social life. Joining clubs or groups centered around your interests can introduce you to new friends and strengthen existing relationships. Sharing a common interest is a great way to build bonds and create a supportive social network.

5. Boosting Self-Esteem and Confidence:

Mastering a new skill or improving at a hobby can significantly boost your self-esteem and confidence. The sense of accomplishment that comes from creating something, learning something new, or improving in a hobby can be incredibly rewarding and empowering.

6. Creating a Balanced Life:

Hobbies help create a balanced life by providing a counterbalance to work and other responsibilities. They offer a way to relax, have fun, and enjoy life outside of your professional obligations. By making time for hobbies, you're investing in your overall well-being and happiness.

Practical Steps to Cultivate Hobbies and Interests.

1. Schedule It:

Just like any other important activity, hobbies need to be scheduled. Make a commitment to yourself by blocking out time in your calendar specifically for your hobbies. Treat this time as non-negotiable, just like a work meeting or doctor's appointment.

2. Start Small:

If you're struggling to find time for hobbies, start small. Even 15 minutes a day dedicated to a hobby can make a difference. As you get used to incorporating this time into your routine, you can gradually increase it.

3. Create a Dedicated Space:

Having a dedicated space for your hobbies can make it easier to engage in them regularly. Whether it's a corner of a room, a spot in your garage, or a space in your garden, having a specific place for your activities can help you get into the right mindset and make it easier to start.

4. *Be Patient:*

Remember, the goal of a hobby is enjoyment and relaxation, not perfection. Be kind to yourself as you advance and progress. Celebrate small victories and don't be too hard on yourself if things don't go perfectly.

5. *Stay Open-Minded:*

Keep an open mind as you explore new hobbies. You might discover interests and talents you never knew you had. Be willing to attempt new things and get out of your comfort zone.

By rediscovering old passions and trying new things, you can enrich your life, reduce stress, and find greater fulfillment. These activities provide a much-needed balance to the demands of work, allowing you to enjoy life more fully. So, take the time to invest in your hobbies and interests. Your well-being, creativity, and overall happiness will thank you for it.

The Joy of Learning Something New.

Imagine waking up every day with a sense of excitement, knowing that you have something enjoyable and stimulating to look forward to outside of your regular work routine. That's the joy of learning something new. It's like discovering a treasure chest filled with limitless possibilities. Whether it's picking up a new language, mastering a musical instrument, or diving into the world of digital art, embracing new hobbies can bring a remarkable sense of fulfillment and happiness to your life.

The Excitement of Discovery.

There's an undeniable thrill in starting something new. Remember the first time you learned to ride a bike or bake a cake? That blend of anticipation, curiosity, and a touch of nervousness is what makes the experience so exhilarating. Learning something new taps into this excitement and adds a refreshing layer of variety to your routine. It breaks the monotony and gives you something to eagerly anticipate.

Boosting Your Confidence.

Each small success in your new hobby boosts your confidence. When you see yourself progressing—whether it's mastering a new chord on the guitar, successfully planting a garden, or completing a challenging puzzle—it instills a sense of accomplishment. This newfound confidence often spills over into other areas of your life, including your professional work. You start to believe in your ability to learn, adapt, and succeed.

Enhancing Your Cognitive Skills.

Learning new things stimulates your brain. It encourages cognitive development and keeps your mind sharp. For instance, learning a new language enhances memory and improves problem-solving skills. Engaging in activities like chess or Sudoku can sharpen your strategic thinking. These mental exercises are not just beneficial for your hobbies but also for your overall cognitive health, helping to delay cognitive decline as you age.

Connecting with Like-minded People.

One of the joys of new hobbies is the opportunity to meet and connect with people who share your interests. Joining a local class, club, or online community can introduce you to a diverse group of people with whom you can share experiences, tips, and encouragement. These social connections can lead to lasting friendships and a broader support network.

Balancing Hobbies with Work and Life.

While the benefits of hobbies are clear, finding the time to pursue them amidst your work and other responsibilities can be challenging. The key lies in balancing your hobbies with work and life in a way that doesn't overwhelm you but instead enriches your daily experience. Here are a few suggestions to balance hobbies with work and life:

Prioritizing Your Interests.

To integrate hobbies into your life, start by prioritizing them. Understand that making time for activities you enjoy is just as important as your professional and personal responsibilities. View your hobbies not as optional extras but as essential components of a balanced life. When you prioritize your interests, you're more likely to find the time to indulge in them.

Time Management Techniques.

Effective time management is crucial for balancing hobbies with work and life. Use techniques like time blocking, where you dedicate specific periods for work, personal responsibilities, and hobbies. Create a weekly schedule that includes dedicated time slots for your hobbies. This structured approach ensures that you regularly engage in activities you love without compromising your work or personal commitments.

Combining Hobbies with Daily Routine.

Look for ways to incorporate your hobbies into your daily routine. If you enjoy reading, carry a book with you and read during your commute or lunch break. If you love gardening, spend a few minutes every morning tending to your plants. Integrating hobbies into your daily routine makes them a natural part of your life, rather than something you have to find extra time for.

Setting Realistic Goals.

It's important to set realistic goals for your hobbies. Understand that you don't have to be perfect or excel immediately. Set small, achievable goals that fit into your schedule. For example, if you're learning to play the piano, aim to practice for 15 minutes a day instead of an hour. This approach prevents you from feeling overwhelmed and allows you to progress at a comfortable pace.

Flexibility and Adaptability.

Life is unpredictable, and sometimes your schedule might not go as planned. Being flexible and adaptable with your hobbies is essential. If you miss a session or don't have time for your hobby one day, don't stress about it. Adjust your schedule and pick it up the next day. The goal is to maintain a positive and enjoyable relationship with your hobbies without adding unnecessary pressure.

Integrating Hobbies with Family and Friends.

Balancing hobbies with work and life becomes easier when you involve your family and friends. Participate in activities that you may all enjoy together. This not only allows you to pursue your interests but also strengthens your relationships. Whether it's cooking a new recipe with your partner, playing a sport with your children, or attending a craft class with friends, shared hobbies can bring joy and deeper connections.

In conclusion, whether you're rediscovering old passions or exploring new ones, hobbies enrich your life, reduce stress, and promote overall well-being. By prioritizing your interests, managing your time effectively, and integrating hobbies into your daily routine, you can achieve a harmonious balance between work and personal life. Remember, the joy of learning something new and balancing hobbies with life is a journey.

Embrace it with an open mind and a positive attitude, and you'll find yourself living a more fulfilled and balanced life.

Reflection Questions: Rediscovering Old Passions

1. What hobbies or interests did you enjoy in your past that you no longer engage in?

Reflect on why you stopped and how those activities made you feel.

2. How did these past hobbies contribute to your happiness and well-being?

Think about the specific ways they added value to your life.

3. What barriers have prevented you from continuing these hobbies?

Consider practical barriers like time and resources, as well as emotional or mental blocks.

4. Which of these old passions still resonate with you today?

Identify the ones that still spark joy or interest in you.

5. How can you reintroduce these passions into your current lifestyle?

Think about small steps or adjustments you can make to include these hobbies again.

Transformative Exercises:

1. Passion Journal:

Create a journal entry listing all the hobbies you enjoyed in the past. Write about how each one made you feel and why you loved it. Reflect on which ones you'd like to revisit.

2. Reconnect with a Past Hobby:

Choose one old hobby and dedicate an hour this week to engage in it. Note how it feels to reconnect with this activity.

3. Vision Board:

Make a vision board with images and words that represent your past passions and how you can incorporate them into your life now.

4. Plan a Revisit:

Set a specific date and time in your calendar to revisit an old hobby. Consider it an essential appointment and commit to it.

Reflection Questions: Trying New Things: Expanding Your Horizons

1. What new activities or hobbies have you been curious about but haven't tried yet?

Reflect on why these activities interest you and what has held you back.

2. How do you feel about stepping out of your comfort zone to try something new?

Consider any fears or anxieties and how you might overcome them.

3. What potential benefits could trying new things bring to your life?

Think about personal growth, joy, and new skills you might acquire.

4. How can you make time in your schedule to explore new hobbies?

Identify specific times or routines that can be adjusted to fit in new activities.

5. What support do you need to start exploring new interests?

Consider if you need encouragement, resources, or companionship to try something new.

Transformative Exercises:

1. New Hobby List:

Write a list of five new hobbies you've always wanted to try. Rank them in order of interest and research local or online classes or resources for each.

2. 30-Day Challenge:

Commit to trying a new hobby for 30 days. Document your experiences, progress, and feelings each day.

3. Join a Class or Group:

Sign up for a class or join a group that focuses on a new interest. Attend at least one session and observe how it feels to engage with others in this new activity.

4. Experiment Week:

Dedicate one week to experimenting with a different new activity each day. Reflect on which ones you enjoyed the most and why.

Reflection Questions: The Joy of Learning Something New

1. What emotions do you experience when you start learning something new?

Reflect on both positive and negative emotions and how they affect your motivation.

2. How has learning new things in the past positively impacted your life?

Think about specific instances where new knowledge or skills have benefited you.

3. What areas of your life could benefit from the joy and excitement of learning something new?

Identify where you feel stagnant and how new learning experiences could revitalize these areas.

4. How do you deal with the challenges and setbacks that come with learning something new?

Consider your coping strategies and how they help or hinder your progress.

5. What are the first steps you can take to start learning something new today?

Outline practical steps you can take immediately to begin a new learning journey.

Transformative Exercises:

1. Learning Diary:

Keep a diary documenting your journey as you learn something new. Write about your successes, challenges, and how the process makes you feel.

2. Mini-Project:

Start a small project related to a new interest. Set clear goals and deadlines to keep yourself motivated and on track.

3. Skill Swap:

Partner with someone who has a skill you want to learn. Offer to teach them something in return, creating a mutually beneficial learning experience.

4. Learning Calendar:

Create a calendar with dedicated time slots for learning something new. Stick to the schedule and review your progress at the end of each week.

Reflection Questions: Balancing Hobbies with Work and Life

1. How do you currently manage your time between work, personal responsibilities, and hobbies?

Reflect on your current balance and identify any areas that need improvement.

2. What challenges do you face in finding time for hobbies?

Consider both external factors (like work demands) and internal factors (like time management skills).

3. How do you feel when you neglect your hobbies due to work or other responsibilities?

Reflect on the emotional and mental impact of not engaging in activities you love.

4. What changes can you make to your daily routine to better balance hobbies with other aspects of your life?

Identify specific actions you can take to create a more balanced schedule.

Transformative Exercises:

1. Time Audit:

Conduct a time audit for one week, noting how you spend each hour of your day. Identify gaps where you can fit in your hobbies and adjust your schedule accordingly.

2. Weekly Hobby Plan:

Create a weekly plan that includes dedicated time slots for your hobbies. Treat these slots as important appointments that you cannot miss.

3. Family and Friends Hobby Night:

Organize a weekly or monthly hobby night with family and friends where everyone engages in their favorite activities together. This encourages social bonding and ensures time for hobbies.

4. Boundary Setting:

Practice setting boundaries by designating certain times as non-negotiable hobby time. Communicate these boundaries clearly to your work and family to ensure they are respected.

CHAPTER NINE.
MINDSET SHIFTS FOR A BALANCED LIFE.

OVERCOMING THE HUSTLE CULTURE.

In the world of today, many of us are caught up in the hustle culture. It's the belief that we must constantly be productive, always striving for more, and pushing ourselves to the limit. This mentality often leads to burnout, stress, and a lack of fulfillment. But what if I told you that there's a better way to live, one that allows you to achieve your goals without sacrificing your well-being?

The hustle culture promotes the idea that your worth is tied to your productivity. You might find yourself feeling guilty for taking breaks or relaxing because you believe you should always be doing something. This mindset is not only unhealthy but also unsustainable in the long run. It's time to challenge this notion and adopt a more balanced approach to life.

Understanding the Hustle Culture.

Hustle culture glorifies constant work and effort, often at the expense of personal health and relationships. It's fueled by social media, where we see influencers and entrepreneurs showcasing their busy lives and accomplishments. The underlying message is that if you're not hustling, you're not succeeding.

This culture can create a sense of inadequacy and pressure, making you feel that you're never doing enough. It can lead to long hours, sacrificing sleep, and neglecting self-care, all in the name of achieving success. However, it's essential to recognize that true success isn't just about professional achievements; it's also about maintaining a healthy, happy, and fulfilling life.

Shifting Your Mindset.

To overcome the hustle culture, you need to start by shifting your mindset. Here are some essential steps to assist you in making this transformation:

1. Redefine Success:

Take a moment to think about your own definition of success. Is it purely about career achievements, or does it include personal happiness, health, and meaningful relationships? Redefining success to include a holistic view of your life can help you prioritize better.

2. Embrace Quality Over Quantity:

Instead of focusing on the number of hours you work, focus on the quality of your work. Are you productive and efficient during your working hours? Are you making substantial progress towards your goals? Quality work often requires periods of rest and rejuvenation.

3. Set Realistic Goals:

It's important to set achievable goals that don't require you to burn the midnight oil constantly. Divide your goals into manageable tasks and celebrate little victories along the way.

This approach reduces stress and keeps you motivated.

4. Learn to Say No:

Overcommitting is a common trait of those entrenched in hustle culture. Learn to say no to tasks and obligations that don't correspond with your priorities. This will free up time for what truly matters to you.

5. Seek Balance:

- Balance doesn't mean giving equal time to work and play every day. It means finding a rhythm that works for you, where you can excel in your career while also enjoying personal time. This balance may vary from day to day, and that's okay.

Implementing the Change.

Changing your mindset isn't an overnight process; it requires consistent effort and practice. Here are some useful recommendations to help you execute these changes:

Create a Balanced Schedule: Plan your day to include work, self-care, and leisure activities. Stick to this schedule as much as possible to ensure you're not neglecting any aspect of your life.

Set Boundaries: Establish clear boundaries between work and personal time. For instance, avoid checking work emails after a certain hour or on weekends. Communicate these boundaries to your colleagues and respect their boundaries as well.

Limit Social Media:

Social media can fuel the hustle culture mentality. Limit your time on these platforms and unfollow accounts that promote an unrealistic, hustle-driven lifestyle. Instead, follow accounts that inspire balance and well-being.

THE IMPORTANCE OF REST AND PLAY.

Rest and play are not just for children; they are essential components of a balanced, fulfilling life. In our quest for productivity, we often overlook the importance of taking breaks and having fun. Yet, rest and play are crucial for our physical, mental, and emotional well-being.

Understanding Rest and Play.

Rest involves taking breaks, getting enough sleep, and allowing your body and mind to recover from daily stressors. Play, on the other hand, involves engaging in activities that bring you joy and stimulate your creativity. Both rest and play are vital for maintaining a healthy balance between work and personal life.

The Science behind Rest and Play.

Numerous studies have shown the benefits of rest and play. Adequate rest improves cognitive function, memory, and mood, while also reducing stress and the risk of burnout. Play, which can include hobbies, sports, or creative activities, enhances problem-solving skills, fosters innovation, and improves overall happiness.

Changing Your Mindset.

To fully embrace the importance of rest and play, you need to shift your mindset and recognize their value.

Here are a few steps to assist you make this change:

1. Acknowledge the Benefits:

Understand that rest and play are not wasted time; they are essential for your well-being and productivity. A properly rested mind is more creative and productive.

2. Prioritize Sleep:

Make sleep a mandatory part of your routine. Aim for 7-9 hours of quality sleep each night. Create a sleep-friendly environment and establish a bedtime routine that helps you unwind.

3. Schedule Breaks:

Incorporate regular breaks into your workday. Short breaks throughout the day can boost your productivity and prevent burnout.

4. Engage in Play:

Make time for hobbies that bring you joy and pleasure. Whether it's playing a sport, painting, gardening, or playing with your pets, these activities can refresh your mind and improve your mood.

5. Disconnect to Reconnect:

Take time to unplug from digital devices and reconnect with yourself and your loved ones. Digital detoxes can reduce stress and help you focus on the present moment.

6. Practice Mindful Rest:

Sometimes, we may feel guilty for resting, thinking we should be doing something productive. Practice mindfulness to fully enjoy your rest periods without guilt. Focus on the present moment and the benefits of resting.

Implementing the Change.

Incorporating rest and play into your life requires intentional effort. Here are some useful tips to assist you in making these changes:

Create a Restful Environment:

Design your bedroom to promote relaxation and sleep. Use comfortable bedding, keep the room cool, and minimize noise and light. Create a nighttime routine that tells your body it's time to wind down.

Plan for Play:

Schedule time for play and leisure activities in your calendar, just as you would for work tasks. Treat these times as important appointments that you cannot miss.

Set Work Boundaries:

Refrain from bringing work into your personal time. Set boundaries around your work hours and stick to them. This might mean not checking emails after a certain hour or turning off work notifications during weekends.

Incorporate Micro-Breaks:

Throughout your workday, take short breaks to relax and rejuvenate. Even a 5-minute walk or stretch can make a big difference in your energy levels.

Explore New Hobbies:

Try out new hobbies and activities that interest you. Exploring different forms of play can help you discover what truly brings you joy and relaxation.

Practice Self-Compassion:

Be kind to yourself if you struggle with taking breaks or having fun. Remember that rest and play are essential for your well-being, and it is okay to prioritize them.

The Benefits of Embracing Rest and Play.

When you prioritize rest and play, you'll start to notice significant improvements in various areas of your life. Here are some of the favorable changes to expect:

Improved Productivity:

Taking regular breaks can enhance your productivity and help you achieve your goals without feeling overwhelmed.

Better Mental Health:

Rest and play reduce stress and anxiety, improving your overall mental health. Engaging in enjoyable activities can boost your mood and provide a sense of accomplishment.

Enhanced Creativity:

Play stimulates your creativity and problem-solving skills. Taking time for hobbies and leisure activities can lead to innovative ideas and solutions.

Stronger Relationships:

Spending quality time with loved ones through play and relaxation strengthens your relationships. It enables you to connect on a deeper level and create lasting memories.

Increased Resilience:

Regular rest and play build your resilience, making you better equipped to handle stress and challenges. When you're well-rested and engaged in enjoyable activities, you're more likely to bounce back from setbacks and approach problems with a positive mindset.

Greater Fulfillment:

Engaging in activities that bring you joy and relaxation leads to a more fulfilling life. You'll feel more satisfied and content, knowing that you're making time for what truly matters.

Work-Life Integration:

Integrating rest and play into your routine helps you achieve a healthier work-life balance. You can excel in your career while also enjoying personal time, leading to a more harmonious life.

Overcoming Obstacles to Rest and Play.

Even with the best intentions, integrating rest and play into your daily life can be challenging. You might face obstacles such as a demanding work schedule, societal pressure to stay busy, or a lack of awareness about the importance of these activities. Here are some useful strategies to help you overcome these barriers:

1. Recognize the Signs of Burnout:

Burnout often manifests as chronic fatigue, irritability, and a lack of motivation. Recognizing these signs can help you understand the importance of taking breaks and engaging in play.

2. Challenge Societal Norms:

Society often glorifies busyness and productivity. Challenge these norms by prioritizing your well-being and setting an example for others. Remember, it's okay to rest and have fun.

3. Educate Yourself and Others:

Learn about the benefits of rest and play and share this knowledge with your peers and colleagues. Educating others can help create a supportive environment where everyone values and prioritizes well-being.

4. Practice Time Management:

Effective time management can help you carve out time for rest and play. Use techniques such as time blocking or setting specific goals to ensure you have time for these essential activities.

5. Address Guilt and Anxiety:

If you feel guilty or anxious about taking breaks or having fun, practice self-compassion and remind yourself of the benefits. Understand that rest and play are not indulgent but necessary for a balanced life.

Integrating Rest and Play into Your Routine.

To make rest and play a regular part of your life, it's important to integrate them into your daily routine. Here are some practical suggestions to help you achieve this:

Morning Routine:

Start your day with activities that promote relaxation and joy. This could include meditation, light exercise, or reading a book. A calm morning routine sets a positive tone for the rest of the day.

Workday Breaks:

Incorporate short breaks into your workday. Stand up, stretch, take a walk, or engage in a quick hobby. These breaks can refresh your mind and boost your productivity.

Evening Wind-Down:

Create a relaxing evening routine to help you unwind after a busy day. This might involve listening to music, practicing mindfulness, or spending time with loved ones.

Weekend Activities:

Dedicate weekends to leisure activities and hobbies. Plan outings, explore new interests, and spend quality time with family and friends. Weekends are an excellent opportunity to recharge.

Vacation and Time Off:

Use your vacation days and time off to rest and engage in enjoyable activities. Travel, explore new places, or simply relax at home. Taking time off is vital for your general well-being.

Conclusion.

In the journey to reclaim your life from work, prioritizing rest and play is crucial. By overcoming the hustle culture mentality and embracing the importance of rest and play, you can achieve a balanced, fulfilling life. It's not about doing less or being less productive; it's about working smarter, not harder, and recognizing the value of self-care and enjoyment.

Remember, success isn't just about professional achievements; it's about living a life that's rich in experiences, relationships, and joy. By making rest and play non-negotiable parts of your routine, you'll be better equipped to handle life's challenges, more creative in your endeavors, and happier overall.

Start today by making small changes to your routine. Take that break, engage in a hobby, and make time for relaxation and fun. Your mind, body, and soul will thank you, and you'll find that you're not just reclaiming your life from work, but truly living it to the fullest.

EMBRACING IMPERFECTION.

When we think about achieving a balanced life, it's easy to get caught up in the pursuit of perfection. We set high standards for ourselves, imagining that only once we reach a state of flawless balance will we be able to relax and truly enjoy life. But here's a little secret: perfection is unreal. Life is inherently messy and unpredictable. Instead of striving for an unattainable ideal, let's explore the power and peace that come from embracing imperfection.

The Perfection Trap.

Many of us fall into the perfection trap without even realizing it. We see it in our endless to-do lists, our meticulously planned schedules, and our constant self-criticism when things don't go as planned. This mindset can be particularly pervasive in our work lives, where there's often pressure to perform flawlessly and meet every expectation.

But perfectionism can be paralyzing. It can lead to burnout, anxiety, and a sense of perpetual dissatisfaction. When we hold ourselves to impossibly high standards, we set ourselves up for failure, because life simply doesn't operate in perfect terms. There will always be unexpected challenges, changes in plans, and moments where we fall short.

Adjusting the Mindset.

So, how do we start embracing imperfection? It begins with a mindset shift—a conscious decision to accept ourselves and our lives as they are, rather than as we think they should be.

We adjust our mindset by:

1. Accepting Human Nature: Understand that being human means being imperfect. We all make mistakes, we all have weaknesses, and we all experience failure. These are not reflections of our worth, but rather of our humanity. By accepting this, we can begin to let go of the unrealistic expectations we place on ourselves.

2. Reframing Failure: Instead of seeing failure as a negative, start viewing it as a valuable part of the learning process. When we embrace failure, we allow ourselves to take risks and innovate without the fear of falling short.

3. Setting Realistic Goals: It's important to set goals that are challenging yet attainable. Break down large tasks into smaller, manageable steps, and celebrate your progress along the way.

4. Prioritizing What Matters: Recognize that not everything requires your best effort. Identify the areas in your life that truly matter and focus your energy there. It's okay to do a "good enough" job on the less important tasks. This way, you can allocate your resources more effectively and avoid spreading yourself too thin.

5. Self-Compassion: Treat yourself with the same kindness and understanding that you would offer to a friend. When you make a mistake or fall short, speak to yourself with compassion rather than criticism. Remember that you are doing your best, and that is enough.

Practical Steps to Embrace Imperfection.

1. Practice Mindfulness: Mindfulness can help you stay present and accept each moment as it comes, without judgment. By cultivating a mindful awareness, you can become more attuned to your thoughts and feelings, and less caught up in the pursuit of perfection.

2. Keep a Gratitude Journal: Each day, write down three things you are grateful for. This practice can shift your focus from what's lacking or imperfect to what's abundant and positive in your life.

3. Set Boundaries: Learn to say no to additional tasks or commitments that will overwhelm you. By setting boundaries, you can protect your time and energy, ensuring that you have enough for the things that truly matter.

4. Seek Support: Surround yourself with supportive people who understand and accept you as you are. Share your struggles and triumphs with them. Their encouragement can help you see the beauty in your imperfections.

GRATITUDE AND POSITIVITY PRACTICES.

In our quest for a balanced life, gratitude and positivity play a crucial role. These practices help us to focus on what is going well, appreciate the good in our lives, and foster a mindset that supports well-being and resilience. Let's explore how cultivating gratitude and positivity can transform our lives and provide practical steps to integrate these practices into our daily routines.

The Power of Gratitude.

Gratitude is the act of recognizing and being thankful the good things in our lives. It redirects our focus from what we lack to what we have, instilling a sense of abundance and contentment.

1. Mental Health Benefits: Research shows that gratitude can enhance mental health by reducing stress, increasing feelings of happiness, and improving overall life satisfaction. When we regularly acknowledge the good in our lives, we train our brains to look for positive experiences, creating a more optimistic outlook.

2. Strengthening Relationships: Expressing gratitude to others strengthens our relationships by making us more connected and empathetic. When we show appreciation for others, it reinforces positive behavior and builds trust and mutual respect.

3. Resilience Building: Gratitude helps us build resilience by enabling us to find silver linings in difficult situations. By focusing on what we are thankful for, even in challenging times, we can maintain a positive attitude and navigate adversity more effectively.

Practical Gratitude Practices.

1. Daily Gratitude Journal: Start or end your day by writing down three things you are grateful for. They can be big or small, from a successful project at work to the warmth of the sun. Reflecting on these moments can uplift your mood and set a positive tone for the day.

2. *Gratitude Letters:* Write a letter to someone who has made a significant impact on your life. Express your appreciation for their support, kindness, or influence. Deliver the letter in person or send it as a heartfelt message. This exercise can deepen your connections and spread positivity.

3. *Gratitude Jar:* Keep a jar in a visible place and fill it with notes of gratitude throughout the week. Whenever you experience something positive, write it down and put it in the jar. At the end of the week, read through the notes to remind yourself of the good things in your life.

4. *Mindful Appreciation:* Throughout the day, take moments to pause and appreciate your surroundings. Whether it's the beauty of nature, a delicious meal, or a kind gesture from a stranger, practice being present and fully experiencing the moment.

The Role of Positivity.

Positivity is more than just a fleeting emotion; it's a mindset that shapes our experiences and interactions. By cultivating positivity, we can enhance our well-being, improve our relationships, and increase our overall satisfaction with life.

1. *Positive Self-Talk:* Our inner dialogue has a powerful impact on how we perceive ourselves and our capabilities. Positive self-talk involves challenging negative thoughts and replacing them with affirming statements. For example, instead of saying, "I can't do this," say, "I am capable and will do my best."

2. *Focus on Strengths:* Rather than dwelling on your weaknesses or failures, focus on your strengths and accomplishments. No matter how small your wins are, be proud of them and use them as a motivation to keep going.

3. *Surround Yourself with Positivity:* The people we spend time with can influence our mindset. Surround yourself with positive, supportive individuals who uplift and inspire you. Take part in activities that make you happy and make you fulfilled.

Practical Positivity Practices.

1. *Positive Affirmations:* Start your day with positive affirmations that reinforce your self-worth and capabilities. Repeat positive affirmations like, "I am confident and able," "I am deserving of love and everything good," or "Today will be a great day."

2. *Visualization:* Spend a few minutes each day visualizing your goals and dreams. Imagine yourself achieving them and experiencing the emotions that come with success. This practice can boost your motivation and create a positive mental framework for achieving your aspirations.

3. *Acts of Kindness:* Perform random acts of kindness for others. It could be as simple as complimenting a colleague, helping a neighbor, or volunteering your time. These acts not only spread positivity but also enhance your own sense of happiness and fulfillment.

4. Positive Media Consumption: Be mindful of the media you consume. Choose content that inspires and uplifts you, whether it's books, podcasts, or movies. Limit exposure to bad news or social media contents that drains your energy.

Integrating Gratitude and Positivity into Your Life.

To make gratitude and positivity a consistent part of your life, consider the following strategies:

1. Create Routine Practices: Integrate gratitude and positivity practices into your daily routine. Consistency is key to making these practices habitual and impactful.

2. Set Reminders: Use reminders to prompt you to practice gratitude and positivity. Set alarms on your phone, place sticky notes around your home, or use apps designed to promote positive thinking.

3. Reflect and Adjust: Regularly reflect on the impact of these practices on your life. Adjust them as needed to keep them fresh and relevant. If one practice becomes routine, try incorporating new techniques to keep things interesting.

4. Share with Others: Encourage friends and family to join you in these practices. Sharing your experiences and supporting each other can enhance the benefits and foster a collective positive mindset.

By embracing imperfection and cultivating gratitude and positivity, you can transform your mindset and create a more balanced, fulfilling life. Remember, it's not about achieving perfection but about appreciating the journey and finding joy in the present moment. As you continue on your path to reclaiming life from work, these mindset shifts will serve as powerful tools to support your well-being and happiness.

Reflection Questions: Overcoming the Hustle Culture.

1. How has the hustle culture impacted your personal and professional life? Are there specific areas where you feel the pressure to constantly be productive?

2. What are some beliefs you hold about success and productivity? Do these beliefs serve you or create unnecessary stress?

3. How do you define a successful day? Is it based solely on accomplishments, or does it include moments of rest and joy?

4. In what ways can you create a healthier work-life balance without feeling guilty about taking breaks?

Transformative Exercises:.

*1. **Intentional Downtime:*** Schedule at least one hour of intentional downtime each day. During this time, engage in activities that relax and rejuvenate you, such as reading, meditating, or simply enjoying a walk in nature.

2. Digital Detox: Designate specific times during the day to disconnect from digital devices. Use this time to engage in offline activities that bring you joy and reduce the constant urge to check emails or social media.

Reflection Questions: The Importance of Rest and Play.

1. How often do you prioritize rest and play in your daily life? What barriers prevent you from doing so?

2. What activities do you find most restful and rejuvenating? How can you incorporate these into your routine more regularly?

3. Reflect on a recent time when you felt truly relaxed and playful. What made that experience special, and how can you recreate it?

4. Do you view rest and play as essential components of a balanced life, or do you see them as indulgences? How can you change this perspective?

5. How does your body signal that it needs rest? Are there physical or emotional cues you often ignore?

Transformative Exercises:

1. Rest Journal: Keep a journal to track your rest patterns for a week. Note how much sleep you get, how rested you feel, and any activities that help you relax. Use this information to identify patterns and make necessary adjustments.

2. Play Calendar: Create a weekly calendar that includes time for playful activities. Choose activities that make you feel joyful and free, such as playing a sport, engaging in a hobby, or spending time with loved ones.

3. Restful Environment: Design a space in your home dedicated to rest and relaxation. Fill it with items that help you unwind, such as comfortable seating, soft lighting, and calming scents.

Reflection Questions: Embracing Imperfection.

1. What areas of your life do you feel the most pressure to be perfect? How does this pressure impact your well-being?

2. Can you recall a time when embracing imperfection led to a positive outcome? How did that experience feel?

3. How do you typically respond to mistakes or failures? Are there ways you can be more compassionate with yourself during these times?

4. What does being "good enough" look like in different areas of your life? How can you practice accepting this standard?

Transformative Exercises:

1. Imperfect Action: Choose an area of your life where you often strive for perfection. Commit to taking action without worrying about achieving a perfect outcome. Ponder on the experience and what you've learned from it.

2. Self-Compassion Practice: When you make a mistake or fall short of your expectations, practice self-compassion. Write a letter to yourself offering understanding and kindness, as you would to a friend in the same situation.

3. Perfection Detox: Choose a week to consciously let go of perfectionism. During this time, allow yourself to make mistakes, take breaks, and prioritize well-being over flawless performance. Reflect on how this detox impacts your stress levels and overall happiness.

Reflection Questions: Gratitude and Positivity Practices.

1. How often do you practice gratitude in your daily life? What obstacles are preventing you from doing so?

2. Can you identify three things you are grateful for today? How does focusing on these things impact your mood and outlook?

3. What role does positivity play in your overall well-being? Are there specific practices that help you maintain a positive mindset?

4. How do you react to negative situations or challenges? Can you find ways to reframe these experiences with a positive perspective?

Transformative Exercises:

1. Gratitude Walk: Take a walk in nature and focus on the things around you that you are grateful for. Notice the beauty of your surroundings, the fresh air, and the peacefulness. Use this time to center yourself and cultivate gratitude.

2. Positivity Challenge: Commit to a 30-day positivity challenge. Each day, engage in an activity that promotes positivity, such as writing a thank-you note, performing a random act of kindness, or sharing a positive story with someone.

3. Gratitude and Positivity Board: Create a visual board filled with images, quotes, and reminders of things you are grateful for and that bring you joy. Place it somewhere you can see daily as a constant reminder of the good in your life.

CHAPTER TEN.
LONG TERM STRATEGIES FOR SUSTAINABLE BALANCE.

SETTING LONG-TERM GOALS.

Achieving a sustainable work-life balance isn't just about making immediate changes; it's also about having a vision for the future and setting long-term goals that align with your values and aspirations. Let's dive into why setting long-term goals is crucial and how you can approach this process in a way that feels motivating and achievable.

Why Long-Term Goals Matter.

Long-term goals provide direction and purpose. They give you something to strive for beyond the daily grind and help you stay focused on what truly matters. Without long-term goals, it's easy to get caught up in the immediate demands of work and life, losing sight of the bigger picture.

Having clear, long-term goals helps you prioritize your time and energy. When you know where you want to be in the future, you can make more informed decisions about how to spend your time now. This clarity can reduce stress and increase your overall sense of fulfillment.

How to Set Effective Long-Term Goals.

1. Reflect on Your Values and Passions: Start by considering what truly matters to you. What are your core values? What activities and pursuits bring you joy and satisfaction? Aligning your long-term goals with your values ensures that they are meaningful and motivating.

2. Visualize Your Ideal Future: Imagine where you want to be in five, ten, or even twenty years. Consider various aspects of your life, including career, personal relationships, health, and personal growth. Visualization helps you create a vivid picture of your goals, making them feel more tangible and achievable.

3. Break Down Your Goals: Long-term goals can feel overwhelming if you view them as one big, distant achievement. Break them down into smaller, manageable milestones. This approach makes the process more manageable and allows you to track your progress over time.

4. Write Down Your Goals: Putting your goals in paper gives them greater substance. It also serves as a reference point that you can revisit and revise as needed. Keep your written goals somewhere visible to remind yourself of what you're working towards.

5. Create an Action Plan: Put together, a step-by-step plan to achieve your goals. Outline the actions you need to take, the resources you'll require, and any potential obstacles you might encounter. An action plan provides a roadmap to guide your efforts.

REGULAR CHECK-INS WITH YOURSELF.

Setting long-term goals is a great start, but maintaining a sustainable work-life balance requires ongoing self-awareness and regular check-ins. These check-ins allow you to assess your progress, celebrate your successes, and make any necessary adjustments to stay on track.

Why Regular Check-Ins Are Important.

Regular check-ins help you stay accountable to yourself. They provide an opportunity to reflect on your actions, evaluate what's working, and identify areas where you might need to make changes. This ongoing process keeps you engaged with your goals and ensures that you're continually moving towards a balanced and fulfilling life.

How to Conduct Effective Check-Ins.

1. Schedule Consistent Check-Ins: Decide on a regular interval for your check-ins, whether it's weekly, monthly, or quarterly. To make this practice a habit, you must be consistent with it.

2. Create a Check-In Routine: Establish a routine for your check-ins. Find a quiet, convenient space where you can think clearly and without interruptions. Consider using a journal to document your thoughts and insights.

3. Review Your Goals: Begin each check-in by revisiting your long-term goals. Reflect on your progress and assess whether you're on track to achieve them. Celebrate any milestones you've reached and acknowledge the effort you've put in.

4. Evaluate Your Actions: Consider the actions you've taken since your last check-in. Are they aligned with your goals? Have you encountered any obstacles or challenges? Reflecting on your actions helps you identify what's working and what might need to change.

5. Assess Your Well-Being: Evaluate your overall well-being, including physical, mental, and emotional health. Are you maintaining a balance between work and personal life? Are there areas where you feel stressed or overwhelmed? Addressing these questions ensures that your pursuit of long-term goals doesn't come at the expense of your well-being.

6. Adjust Your Plans: Based on your reflections, make any necessary adjustments to your action plan. This might involve revising your goals, changing your approach, or seeking additional support. Flexibility is essential to staying adaptable and resilient.

7. Set Short-Term Goals: Use your check-ins to set short-term goals that will move you closer to your long-term objectives. These smaller goals provide immediate focus and motivation, making the journey more manageable.

ADAPTING TO LIFE CHANGES.

Creating a sustainable work-life balance is not about achieving a perfect equilibrium every day, but rather about developing long-term strategies that allow you to adapt to life's inevitable changes and celebrate your progress along the way.

Life is constantly evolving, bringing new challenges and opportunities. Whether it's a change in your career, family dynamics, health, or personal interests, adapting to these changes is crucial for maintaining a sustainable work-life balance. Let's dig into how you can navigate these changes effectively and maintain balance.

1. *Embracing Flexibility:*

Flexibility is key to adapting to life's changes. A rigid approach to balancing work and life can lead to frustration and burnout when unexpected events occur. Embracing flexibility allows you to adjust your routine and priorities as needed.

Strategies for Flexibility

1. Create Buffer Times: Build buffer times into your schedule to accommodate unexpected tasks or emergencies. This helps prevent your day from becoming overloaded and gives you the space to handle surprises without stress.

2. Set Priorities: Identify your top priorities each day. This ensures that even if your schedule changes, the most important tasks are still addressed. Setting priorities aids in keeping your attention on the important things.

3. Stay Open-Minded: Be open to new opportunities and changes. Sometimes, unexpected changes can lead to new and exciting possibilities. Embracing an open-minded attitude can turn challenges into opportunities for growth.

4. Practice Mindfulness: Mindfulness helps you stay present and adaptable. By focusing on the present moment, you can better handle changes and make thoughtful decisions. Regular mindfulness practice can improve your ability to stay calm and flexible.

2. Regular Self-Reflection:

Regularly reflecting on your current situation and your work-life balance can help you stay on track and make necessary adjustments. Self-reflection allows you to assess your progress, identify areas for improvement, and celebrate your successes.

Self-Reflection Practices.

1. Daily Check-Ins: Take a few minutes each day to reflect on your accomplishments and challenges. Ask yourself what went well and what could be improved. Daily check-ins help you stay aware of your progress and maintain focus.

2. Weekly Reviews: At the end of each week, review your schedule and goals. Assess your progress and make adjustments for the coming week. Weekly reviews provide a broader perspective on your balance and help you stay aligned with your goals.

3. Monthly Assessments: Once a month, conduct a more in-depth review of your work-life balance. Evaluate your long-term goals and determine if any changes are needed to stay aligned with them. Monthly assessments help you stay committed to your vision.

3. Developing Resilience:

Resilience is the ability to recover from setbacks and adjust to change. It's a crucial skill for maintaining a sustainable work-life balance. Building resilience helps you navigate life's ups and downs with confidence and grace.

Strategies for Building Resilience.

1. Stay Positive: Focus on positive aspects of your life and work. This mindset helps you navigate challenges more effectively. Cultivating a positive outlook can boost your resilience and overall well-being.

2. Learn from Experiences: View setbacks as learning opportunities. Reflect on what you can improve and how you can handle similar situations better in the future. Learning from experiences helps you grow stronger and more adaptable.

3. Seek Support: Lean on your support system during difficult times. Whether it's family, friends, or colleagues, having a strong network can provide emotional and practical support. Building and maintaining relationships is essential for resilience.

4. Practice Self-Care: Prioritize self-care to maintain your physical and mental health. Regular exercise, healthy eating, adequate sleep, and relaxation techniques can strengthen your resilience. Self-care is a fundamental part of staying balanced and adaptable.

4. Anticipating Life Changes:

Some life changes are predictable, such as aging, career transitions, or family growth. Anticipating these changes can help you prepare and adjust your work-life balance proactively. Planning ahead allows you to navigate transitions smoothly and maintain balance.

Planning for Predictable Changes:

1. Career Transitions: If you're planning a career change or advancement, consider how it will impact your work-life balance. Prepare by updating your skills and planning your career path. Proactively managing career transitions helps you stay balanced and focused.

2. Family Changes: Whether you're planning to start a family or your children are growing up, anticipate how these changes will affect your routine and responsibilities. Adjusting your schedule and seeking support can help you manage family transitions effectively.

3. Health and Wellness: Prioritize your health and wellness by incorporating regular exercise, healthy eating, and preventive care into your routine. Anticipating health needs can help you stay balanced in the long term. Regular check-ups and a proactive approach to health can prevent future disruptions.

4. Personal Growth: Plan for personal growth and development. Whether it's pursuing a new hobby, continuing education, or self-improvement, integrating personal growth into your long-term plans ensures you stay fulfilled and balanced.

CELEBRATING YOUR WINS.

Acknowledging and celebrating your successes is essential for maintaining motivation and a positive mindset. Celebrating wins, both big and small, reinforces your commitment to work-life balance and helps you stay on track.

Recognizing Achievements

Recognizing your achievements, no matter how minor they may seem, can boost your morale and encourage you to keep striving for balance. Celebrating your progress fosters a sense of accomplishment and reinforces positive behaviors.

Ways to Recognize Achievements:

1. Daily Acknowledgment: At the end of each day, take a moment to acknowledge what you've accomplished. This can be as simple as writing down three things you did well. Daily acknowledgment helps you stay positive and motivated.

2. Milestone Celebrations: Set milestones for your long-term goals and celebrate when you reach them. This could be completing a project, sticking to a new habit for a month, or achieving a personal goal. Celebrating milestones reinforces your commitment and progress.

3. Share Your Success: Share your achievements with friends, family, or colleagues. Celebrating together can enhance your sense of accomplishment and provide additional encouragement. Sharing success builds a supportive community and strengthens relationships.

Creating a Reward System

Establishing a reward system for yourself can make the process of maintaining work-life balance more enjoyable and motivating. Rewards provide positive reinforcement and keep you focused on your goals.

Designing a Reward System:

1. Identify Rewards: Choose rewards that are meaningful and enjoyable for you. This could be anything from a relaxing day off, a favorite treat, or a special activity. Personalizing rewards makes them more motivating and enjoyable.

2. Set Criteria: Determine the criteria for earning rewards. This could be completing a specific task, reaching a milestone, or maintaining a new habit for a certain period. Clear criteria provide structure and clarity for your reward system.

3. Celebrate Regularly: Make celebrating a regular part of your routine. Regular rewards keep you motivated and remind you of the progress you're making. Consistent celebrations reinforce positive behaviors and maintain motivation.

Balancing Self-Care and Celebration

Celebrating your wins is an important aspect of self-care. Balancing self-care with celebrations helps you stay energized and motivated in your journey towards sustainable work-life balance.

Integrating Self-Care and Celebration

1. Self-Care Activities: Plan self-care activities that also serve as celebrations. This could be a spa day, a relaxing bath, or a favorite hobby. Combining self-care and celebration ensures you prioritize your well-being.

2. Mindful Celebrations: Practice mindfulness during your celebrations. Be fully present and savor the moment, appreciating the effort and progress you've made. Mindful celebrations enhance your enjoyment and reinforce positive experiences.

3. Balanced Indulgence: Treat yourself without overindulging. Balance celebrations with healthy habits to maintain your overall well-being. Balanced indulgence ensures you enjoy rewards without compromising your health.

As you continue your journey towards sustainable work-life balance, remember that it's not about perfection, but progress. Celebrate your successes, learn from your challenges, and stay committed to your goals. With intention and effort, you can create a life that is fulfilling, balanced, and uniquely yours.

Practical Exercises for Long-Term Balance

To help you implement these long-term strategies, here are some practical exercises you can incorporate into your routine:

1. Goal Setting Exercise: Write down your long-term work-life balance goals. Break them down into smaller, actionable steps and set deadlines for each step. Review and adjust your goals regularly to stay on track.

2. Flexibility Practice: Identify one area of your life where you can practice more flexibility. Experiment with different approaches and reflect on the outcomes. This practice helps you develop a flexible mindset.

3. Support System Check-In: Schedule regular check-ins with your support network. Discuss your progress, challenges, and how you can support each other. Building strong connections strengthens your support system.

4. Gratitude Journal: Keep a gratitude journal and write down three things you're grateful for each day. Reflecting on positive aspects of your life enhances your overall well-being and reinforces a positive mindset.

5. Milestone Celebration Plan: Plan how you will celebrate when you reach specific milestones in your work-life balance journey. Having a celebration plan in place keeps you motivated and excited about your progress.

By incorporating these exercises into your routine, you can reinforce your commitment to long-term balance and make meaningful progress towards a sustainable, fulfilling life. Remember, balance is a journey, not a destination. Stay patient, stay positive, and enjoy the journey towards reclaiming your life from work.

Reflection Questions: Setting Long-Term Goals.

1. What are your long-term goals for achieving work-life balance?

Reflect on the vision you have for your future in terms of balancing work and personal life. What specific outcomes do you desire?

2. How do your current habits and routines support or hinder your long-term goals?

Think about the ways in which your daily actions align with your long-term goals. Are there any habits you need to change or develop?

3. What resources and support systems do you need to achieve your long-term goals?

Think about the tools, knowledge, and people that can help you reach your goals. How can you leverage these resources?

Transformative Exercises:

1. Goal Mapping:

Create a detailed map of your long-term goals. Break them down into smaller, manageable steps and set deadlines for each milestone. Visualize your path to success.

2. Future Self Letter:

Write a letter to your future self, detailing your goals and the changes you want to see in your life. Read this letter periodically to remind yourself of your long-term vision.

Reflection Questions: Regular Check-Ins with Yourself.

1. How often do you take time to reflect on your work-life balance?

Reflect on the frequency and quality of your self-assessments. Are you consistent in checking in with yourself?

2. What questions do you ask yourself during these check-ins?

Consider the types of questions that help you evaluate your progress and well-being. Are they effective in providing clarity?

3. How do you feel after a regular check-in with yourself?

Reflect on the emotions and insights you experience after taking time to self-assess. How does it impact your motivation and direction?

4. What changes have you made based on your self-assessments?

Think about the adjustments you've implemented after reflecting on your work-life balance. Have these changes been beneficial?

Transformative Exercises:

1. Self-Reflection Journal:

Start a self-reflection journal where you record your thoughts, feelings, and progress on work-life balance. Schedule regular times for journaling, such as weekly or monthly.

2. Mindfulness Meditation:

Integrate mindfulness meditation into your routine to improve self-awareness. Use this practice to check in with your thoughts, emotions, and physical sensations.

Reflection Questions: Adapting to life Changes

1. How do you usually respond to significant changes in your life?

Reflect on your natural reactions to major life events and transitions. Are you adaptable or resistant to change?

2. What recent life changes have impacted your work-life balance?

Consider the events or transitions that have disrupted your routine. How have they affected your ability to maintain balance?

3. What strategies have you used to adapt to these changes?

Think about the coping mechanisms and adjustments you've employed. Which strategies have been effective?

4. How can you better prepare for future changes?

Reflect on the steps you can take to become more resilient and adaptable. What proactive measures can you implement?

Transformative Exercises:

1. Change Management Plan:

Develop a change management plan for potential future disruptions. Outline steps you can take to adapt quickly and maintain balance.

2. Reflective Adaptation Exercise:

Reflect on a past life change and how you adapted to it. Write down the lessons learned and how you can apply them to future situations.

Reflection Questions: Celebrating Your Wins.

1. How often do you take time to celebrate your achievements, big or small?

Reflect on your habits regarding acknowledging and celebrating your successes. Are you quick to move on without recognizing your efforts?

2. How does celebrating your wins impact your motivation and morale?

Reflect on the effects of celebration on your overall well-being and drive. Does it encourage you to keep going and maintain balance?

3. What prevents you from celebrating your successes more frequently?

Think about the barriers that keep you from taking time to acknowledge your achievements. Are these barriers internal, such as self-criticism, or external, like lack of time?

Transformative Exercises:

1. Win Jar:

Start a win jar where you write down your achievements on slips of paper and place them in a jar. At the end of each month, read through them and celebrate your progress.

2. Celebration Ritual:

Develop a personal celebration ritual that you perform whenever you achieve a goal. This could be treating yourself to something special, taking a day off, or doing an activity you love.

3. Achievement Reflection:

Set aside time each week to reflect on what you've accomplished. Write down your wins in a journal and note how they contribute to your long-term goals.

CONCLUSION.
REFLECTING ON YOUR JOURNEY.

As we come to the end of this book, it's time to pause and reflect on the journey we've undertaken together. Think back to the beginning, when you first picked up this book. What motivated you to start reading about reclaiming your life from work? Was it a feeling of overwhelm, a desire for more balance, or perhaps a nudge from someone who cares about you? Whatever brought you here, it's worth acknowledging the courage it took to embark on this journey.

Throughout these chapters, we've explored various facets of work-life balance, digging into practical tips and strategies designed to help you regain control over your time and energy. We've talked about breaking down your day, finding the gaps, and creating a schedule that works for you. You've learned about the Pomodoro Technique and other hacks to boost productivity and manage interruptions gracefully. We've discussed the importance of setting boundaries, unplugging, and saying no without guilt. You've explored the essentials of self-care, both physical and mental, and the critical role of a support system in your life.

Now, take a moment to reflect on what you've learned and how you've applied these insights to your life. Have you noticed any changes in how you go about your daily routine? Are you more mindful of how you spend your time? Have you set clearer boundaries with work, and are you feeling more present with your loved ones? Reflect on these questions and recognize the progress you've made, no matter how small. Every step forward is a victory in reclaiming your life.

CONTINUING TO GROW AND EVOLVE.

Your journey doesn't end here. In fact, this is just the beginning. Achieving a balanced life is not a one-time event but an ongoing process that requires continuous growth and adaptation. Life is dynamic, and as you encounter new challenges and opportunities, your approach to work-life balance will need to evolve.

One of the key takeaways from this book is the importance of regular self-reflection. Make it a habit to check in with yourself frequently. Ask yourself how you're feeling, what areas of your life need more attention, and what adjustments you can make to stay on track. Growth comes from this ongoing process of self-awareness and course correction.

It's also important to stay open to learning and trying new things. The strategies that work for you now might need to be tweaked or replaced as your circumstances change.

Have an open mind and always be willing to try out new ideas and different strategies. Stay curious and keep exploring ways to improve your work-life balance.

Remember, this journey is uniquely yours. While it's valuable to learn from others and gather insights from books and mentors, ultimately, you need to find what works best for you. Trust yourself and be patient.

Growth takes time, and it's absolutely acceptable to make mistakes along the way. Each misstep provides an opportunity to learn and progress.

Encouraging Others to Reclaim Their Lives.

As you continue on your path to a balanced life, consider how you can support others in their journey. Work-life balance is not just a personal issue; it's a societal one. By encouraging and helping others, you contribute to a larger movement towards healthier, more balanced lives for everyone.

Start by sharing your experiences and insights with those around you. Talk to your friends, family, and colleagues about what you've learned and how it's impacted your life. Sometimes, a simple conversation can spark significant change in someone else's life. Be open about your struggles and successes, and offer practical advice and encouragement.

If you're in a leadership position at work, think about how you can establish a culture of balance and well-being. Advocate for policies that support work-life balance, such as flexible working hours, remote work options, and mental health resources. Lead by example by setting boundaries and prioritizing self-care.

Your actions have the potential to encourage others to do the same.

Consider also the power of community. Join or start a support group focused on work-life balance. These groups can provide a safe space for sharing experiences, offering support, and holding each other accountable. There's strength in numbers, and together, you can achieve more than you could alone.

FINAL WORDS OF WISDOM.

As we conclude this book, I want to leave you with a few final words of wisdom. First and foremost, always keep in mind that you are not alone. Many people are navigating the challenges of balancing work and personal life, and it is okay to ask for help when you need it. Reach out to your support system and lean on them. There's no shame in seeking assistance, whether it's from friends, family, or professionals.

Secondly, be kind to yourself. It's easy to be your harshest critic, but self-compassion is crucial. Understand that perfection is unattainable, and it's okay to have off days.

Celebrate your successes, no matter how little, and learn from your setbacks. Treat yourself with the same love and understanding that you would extend to a friend.

Lastly, stay true to your values. In the hustle and bustle of daily life, it's easy to lose sight of what truly matters to you. Regularly reconnect with your core values and let them guide your decisions. Whether it's spending time with loved ones, pursuing a passion, or taking care of your health, make sure your actions align with what you hold dear.

In conclusion, reclaiming your life from work is a deeply personal and transformative journey. It's about finding balance, setting boundaries, practicing self-care, and building a supportive community. It's about continuously growing and evolving while staying true to your values. And most importantly, it's about living a life that feels fulfilling and meaningful to you.

Thank you for letting me to be part of your journey. I hope the insights and strategies shared in this book have inspired you and provided you with practical tools to reclaim your life from work. Remember, you have the ability to create the balance you seek, and with determination and self-compassion, you can achieve it. Here's to living a balanced, fulfilling, and joyful life.

HOW WAS IT?

Dear Reader,

Thank you for embarking on the journey through "The Ultimate Guide to Reclaiming Life from Work: Step-by-step Strategies for Liberation from Work's Grip." Your time and dedication to improving your work-life balance mean the world to me. I hope this guide has provided you with valuable insights and practical strategies to regain control of your life.

If you found this book helpful, I would be incredibly grateful if you could take a moment to rate and leave a review on Amazon. Your feedback not only helps other readers discover the book but also supports the ongoing mission to empower more people to reclaim their lives from the demands of work.

Thank you once again for your support and for taking the first steps towards a more balanced and fulfilling life.

Warmest regards,

Ruth Kings.

www.ingramcontent.com/pod-product-compliance
Lightning Source LLC
Chambersburg PA
CBHW071916210526
45479CB00002B/437